WHAT THEY ARE

Keith stands up to his title of the UK's #1 Fear Strategist. A fascinating man, with amazing stories to tell.

— BRAD BURTON, FOUNDER OF 4NETWORKING

You just don't know, what you don't know. And sometimes someone comes along and all of a sudden, it makes sense. An epiphany, a lightbulb moment. They don't do the work for you but they guide you on the path. My deepest thanks to that someone who is the author of this very book that you hold in your hand. I truly hope you get as much from reading and working through this book as I did. Thank you Keith for lighting the way.

— MISS H WHYMENT-LESTER, BUSINESS MANAGER, LONDON

Keith writes honestly and candidly and speaks directly to the reader with great effect. I found the book both thought provoking and informative, yet written in a way which made it easy to read.

— JOANNA MICHAEL, UK

I've seen Keith talk at many different networking events and learnt something different each time. This book not only reinforces those lessons but teaches me more. Thank you Keith.

— GARY JONES, GROW MARKETING AND MEDIA

Do you want to be authentic? Then *The Masks We Wear* is an eye-opening, potent read for you. Throughout the book you discover masks you wear unconsciously. Once they are removed you can relax into who you are and express your uniqueness; people can really get to know you, and deep and honest relationships can be built. Unmask and enjoy life!

— ANTONIA OLGA DANIEK - FOUNDER OF "BE THE CHANGE-MAKER"

Words aren't my best way of communication. For me it's about feelings, and this man and this book deffo gets me right in the feels. Keith is not only a wonderful inspiring eloquent speaker but also a wonderful man and friend. He's definitely helped me on more than one occasion and now with this book I have a little bit of him in my home as well as my heart.

— MISS AMY TEMPLE, FEMALE EMPOWERER

Keith Blakemore-Noble's understanding of the intricacies and interplay of people's fears and emotions are very apparent throughout this excellent text.

Combined with the experience and practical knowledge Keith has gathered over many years - and through his personal professional practice, he is ideally placed and personally qualified to explore and write about this interesting topic.

A must read for those interested to discover more about the metaphorical masks that each of us wear (at least at one time or another), their importance, and what to do about them.

— ALISON STEAD, COUNSELLOR (ADV.DIP.COUNS)

I had the pleasure of being one of the first people to read this book, and while the subject can be a bit scary for some, I honestly believe it will be a great help to many. Keith has a way of making quite a difficult subject seem very easy to understand and to work through.

This book deserves your time, your attention and your best.

And you deserve this book.

— PAUL NEWTON, MENTALTHEFT

THE MASKS
WE WEAR

To Shirley,

Looking forward to seeing you embrace life without masks!

All the best,

Kent

ALSO BY KEITH BLAKEMORE-NOBLE

Winning In Life And Work series -

Winning In Life And Work : Volume 1 (*Be Your Change, 2013*)

Winning in Life and Work : New Beginnings (*Be Your Change, 2015*)

Winning in Life and Work : Success Secrets (*Be Your Change, 2017*)

Winning in Life and Work : Dare To Dream (*Be Your Change, 2019*)

The Complete Almost Everything You Always Wanted To Know About Phobias (but were afraid to ask) (*Be Your Change, due 2021*)

Keith has also contributed to the following books -

Ready, Aim, Captivate! (*Experts Insights Publishing, 2012*)

The Inspiration Bible (*Gowor International Publishing, 2014*)

Unsung Heroes : Deconstructing Suicide Through Stories Of Triumph (*UnSung Hero Publishing, 2016*)

You can find out more details about all of Keith's books (existing and forthcoming, as well as the ones to which he has contributed) at KeithBlakemoreNoble.com/books/author/

THE MASKS WE WEAR

KEITH BLAKEMORE-NOBLE
THE UK'S #1 FEAR STRATEGIST

Be Your Change
An imprint of Keith Blakemore-Noble Ltd

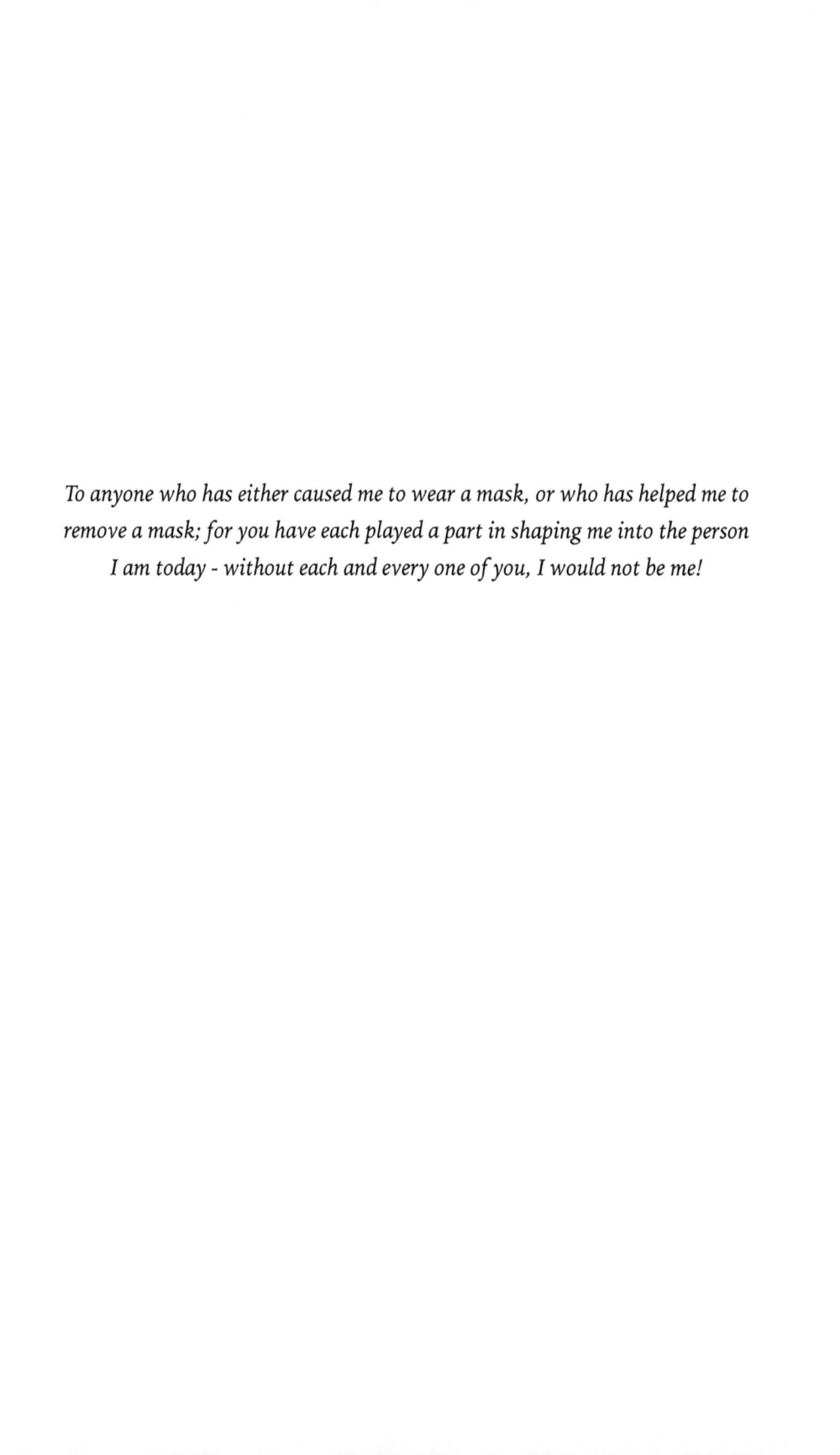

To anyone who has either caused me to wear a mask, or who has helped me to remove a mask; for you have each played a part in shaping me into the person I am today - without each and every one of you, I would not be me!

"No man, for any considerable period, can wear one face to himself and another to the multitude, without finally getting bewildered as to which may be the true."

— NATHANIEL HAWTHORNE, THE SCARLET LETTER

Copyright © 2020 by Keith Blakemore-Noble

All rights reserved.

No part of this book may be reproduced in any form or by any electronic or mechanical means, including information storage and retrieval systems, without written permission from the author, except for the use of brief quotations in a book review.

First Printing 2020

Paperback ISBN: 978-0-9931625-8-9

eBook ISBN: 978-0-9931625-9-6

Published by Be Your Change – Be-Your-Change.co.uk.

Be Your Change is an imprint of Keith Blakemore-Noble Ltd - KeithBlakemoreNoble.com

British Library Cataloguing-in-Publication Data

A catalogue record for this book is available from the British Library.

Bonus Word : liberator

ACKNOWLEDGMENTS

No man is an island, as the old saying goes, and this book could not have happened without the help of many people to whom I am greatly indebted -

- My beta readers Gary Jones, Helena Whyment-Lester, Joanna Mitchell, and Paul Newton for their wonderful support and their very helpful feedback.
- My editor Alison Reeves for doing a great job of catching my numerous typos, misspellings, and grammatical faux pas.
- My designer Simon Clements for taking my very vague rough ideas for the cover and turning them into something sumptuously gorgeous and way beyond my wildest dreams.
- Christina Kokis for her gentle nudge back in April which lead to this book's creation (it was she who persuaded me that there was merit in expanding the original talk).
- Elliot Kay who christened my Mask Talk (read the Preface

to see what that's about!) which got the cogs whirring and set things on the initial path all those years ago.
- My ex-wife for being such an understanding lady at the time, and for turning into the amazing woman she is today.
- My partner Callum Widdowson for always being there for me, for being very supportive throughout, and generally for just being awesome.
- And last, but by no means least, to you dear reader - for without you there would have been no point in creating this book at all.

CONTENTS

Preface — xvii
Introduction — xxiii

Prologue — 1

Part I
INTRODUCING YOUR MASKS

1. What Is A Mask? — 7
2. Why Do We Wear Masks? — 11
3. Where Do They Come From? — 17
4. What Happens When We Wear A Mask? — 23
5. What Happens When We Take It Off? — 29

Part II
RELEASING YOUR MASKS

6. How Do We Take Them Off? — 37
7. A Simple Question — 43
8. Going Deeper — 47
9. Dealing With The Fear — 53
10. Return Of The Mask? — 65

Part III
BEYOND YOUR MASKS

11. A New Life — 77
12. 8 Powerful Words — 89
13. A Useful Anchor — 95
14. When Is A Mask Not A Mask? — 101
15. Where To Now? — 107

Epilogue — 111
Need A Little Help? — 115

About the Author — 119

PREFACE

The Masks We Wear has had a long and varied gestation, stretching back at least eight years.

It started as a nice attention-grabbing introduction to a very different talk I gave during at one meeting of a Speaking Club of which I was a member in London.

I gave a 10-minute talk around equality and the benefits of recognising and celebrating our differences, and I wanted something very visual with which to open the talk and grab everyone's attention from the outset.

I hit upon the idea of starting the talk wearing a mask. Unfortunately, I only hit upon the idea as I was travelling to London ready to give the talk! The only mask I managed to find was an Iron Man mask, and so that's what opened the talk.

Response to the talk was overall good and people enjoyed the mask opening, although many felt confused - "What does Iron Man have to do with it?" They did make a very good point!

A year or so later I was at another training event, and this required us all to deliver a talk. I decided to resurrect the talk I'd done a year earlier, and I asked a fellow attendee Elliot if he had something I could borrow with which to make an impromptu mask. Elliot was one of those people who is always prepared for absolutely anything, so if anyone could help create an impromptu mask, it would be him!

"Oh, are you doing your Mask Talk?" he asked - and suddenly I had A Talk! Not just a talk which could be wheeled out, but A Talk which was still stuck in someone's mind a year later! Of course, at this stage the mask was still really just a prop for opening the talk, but the seed was sown...

Over the next few years, various speaking opportunities came along, which I always grasped with both hands of course. And during this time, that talk started to evolve.

There were two main driving factors which contributed to this evolution.

The first was the general reception to the overall talk - the mask aspect seemed to be the one which generated most interest, the one which people remembered the most, and the one which engaged far more than the rest of the talk. In fact, by this stage, the opening gimmick was overshadowing the rest of the talk. Clearly a sign.

The second was that during the intervening years, as I continued to specialise in helping people to conquer their fears and phobias, I was becoming more and more aware of the various masks which we all wear as part of our attempts to protect ourselves from our fears.

On reflection, it was inevitable that the masks component of the talk would take over. This was sealed when I started exploring some techniques for helping people get back in touch with their authentic inner selves. Indeed, it was from this aspect that the term *"8 Powerful Words"* was born - mainly because there are eight very powerful words which form a key part of that journey. We explore the concept of these words in a chapter in this book, although it will have a far greater impact for you if you work through the book in order, so that when you reach the chapter, you have everything in place to get the best from it. As they say, the best things are worth waiting for.

And so it was that my talk *"8 Powerful Words"* was born, bringing all these aspects together.

I delivered this talk a few times, always to a great reception.

So, when I got more heavily involved with a massive networking organisation, one which invites a member to give an 18 minute talk (which is, they are at pains to point out, not a sales pitch - that catches a lot of people out), I immediately thought of 8 Powerful Words and duly delivered it at one meeting.

The response was amazing, I got so many supportive comments from people who heard it.

And then something amazing happened. I started getting asked to come and deliver it to different people at more and more of their meetings. Over the course of the next eight weeks, I gave the talk 22 times.

Every time, I would get lots of great feedback from people, many people opening up and sharing how they suddenly realised a massive thing for their lives, and the difference it was making just to realise they were wearing masks.

What really blew me away though, was when I discovered that some people were attending meetings specifically to hear that talk more than once. One person told me that they had heard it four times, and they had chosen those particular meetings to attend (there are 80 or more meetings a week from which to choose) specifically to hear "*8 Powerful Words*" again and again as they got something more from it each time.

After a while I got people asking if there was more, what they could do next on their journey, and so (with a little gentle encouragement from one person in particular), the idea for this book was born.

Of course, it couldn't be called *8 Powerful Words* - that works well as a talk title, but would just get lost in the general noise as a book title. And to be fair, the book goes way beyond what the talk covers anyway.

I came up with about a dozen different possible titles, discussed it with peers, floated the different titles past groups who had heard the talk and groups who hadn't. And a strong consensus formed with one particular title so far ahead of all the others in popularity that there really was no alternative. Thankfully, it was the original working title I'd created for the book, which was a very gratifying moment.

Thus began this book which you hold in your hand (or view on your computer, or listen to on - oh, you know what I mean).

On the one hand, it was written over the course of a few weeks (having delivered the talk 22 times before starting to write this book really helped - you can't beat sharing your ideas with hundreds of people and getting real-time feedback on which bits resonate and which bits confuse). On the other hand, this book is eight years in the making. Although one might even say it's been 54 years in the making.

However, you count its gestation, the important thing is that I hope you find it interesting, illuminating, and inspiring.

My wish is that by reading this book, you start to get an awareness of, and a deeper understanding of, the masks we wear, and that you are able to take this knowledge and use it to create for yourself an even better and more enjoyable life ahead.

Keith Blakemore-Noble

Keith Blakemore-Noble
Scotland
31st May 2020

INTRODUCTION

Get ready for a journey of self-discovery, perhaps in a way in which you've never journeyed before.

As you've probably spotted from the Contents page, this book is split in to three main sections, each one focusing on a specific facet of the masks we wear.

The first section, Introducing Your Mask, introduces us to the concept of masks, defines what they are, explores where they come from, and exams why we choose (for it is a choice, albeit often an unconscious one) to wear them. It also takes a look at what happens as we remove them, addressing the most common fears people have about removing their masks - for such removal can indeed be scary, but it is ultimately very empowering and certainly very worth our while doing.

The second section, Releasing Your Mask, deals (as you might expect) with how we go about releasing and removing our masks now that we have decided it's time for them to go. We look at several different ways in which we can loosen and remove our masks, exploring how that works in different contexts. We examine the fears which can arise from removing our masks and look at how we can overcome those fears. We finish this section by considering the biggest question of all, namely will our masks return, or are we free of them forever?

In the third section, Beyond Your Masks, we explore what life brings us once we've removed our masks. We take a look at just how powerful this can be, we explore how we can help ourselves to keep the masks away, we examine the differences between masks and our various personas, and we take a look at the important question of where we go from here.

This book is very much sequential in nature and design - it is designed to be read from start to finish, rather than to be dipped into at random, and the reader is strongly encouraged to read it in that order.

Many readers will find that they also get great benefit from rereading the entire book from time to time - this is very much by design. As we move through our own lives and follow our own particular paths, so our understanding of our situation changes and evolves. Which is the same with both masks and this book.

When you re-read the book, you will be reading it from a different perspective, with changed experiences, and very often that can and does bring out new meaning, new insight, and new understanding.

Again, because of the sequential nature of the book, with each chapter building upon the previous, and each section likewise in turn, re-reading the book will produce the greatest reward when it is done in its entirety, rather than just dipping in, although of course that is entirely at the reader's discretion.

It would be prudent at this point, however, to sound a note of caution, which is best summed up seven words:

There is no "one size fits all".

We know the clothes label "one size fits all" lies; there are plenty of people it will not fit.

The same is true for everything in life.

Which includes how to grow your business, improve your life, conquer your fears, etc.

Sadly there are far too many people who will swear blind that they have The One True Way, and that if you follow their steps exactly (and only their steps) you will get whatever results you are seeking.

And many people get taken in by this.

Unfortunately, while it is true that those steps will work for some, they will not work for everyone.

We are all different; different people have different needs, different ways of working, and get different results even when doing the same thing.

Which is why it's important for any competent expert with whom you work to recognise this and to make sure they tailor the solution to you and your specific situation.

A good expert will take time to work with you up front to fully understand your situation, your needs, the way you work, etc, BEFORE they prescribe the optimal solution.

Beware of anyone who just dives straight in with "all the answers" without considering your situation, especially when they use the same approach with everyone.

One size definitely does not fit all.

"That's all well and good Keith, but what has this got to do with this book?" I hear you ask.

While writing this book, I have been conscious that not everything will work for everyone. Because there will be a wide variety of readers, it has been important to make sure as many possibilities are covered as possible.

All of which means that when you read this book, and especially when you get a little deeper into some of the chapters, you may feel that some of the examples or even some of the exercises don't seem to fit for you. That's absolutely fine. Go with them the best you can. Mull them over, see what could be changed for them to fit your personal situation better. Then either go with them in that form or move on to the next one (where there are exercises or suggestions offered, I've attempted to make several to cover as many possibilities as I can).

Above all, don't worry if one piece doesn't quite seem to gel for you, that's perfectly natural, just notice it, recognise that one-size does not fit all, and move along to the next piece.

Always remember to put everything into it - the more you put in, the greater your outcome and results will be.

Oh yes - and have fun!

PROLOGUE

Come with me, if you will, on a journey - a journey all the way back to when I was young, and the world was black and white.

My first five years were spent growing up pretty much in the middle of nowhere, in a farmhouse in rural Aberdeenshire in the North-East of Scotland.

It was just me, my mum, my dad, and the radio. My sister came along when I was three, but it was just us. I didn't really have much contact with other people, especially not other children, so I didn't really learn how to interact with other people. I did learn how to interact with the radio, but it turns out that you can't just retune people when you get bored of them as that is considered rude.

Once I reach the age of five, we moved to a small village of about 600 people, and that is where I went to school.

So it was on my first day of school that I turned up and there were loads of other children my age and older. Many of them were playing. Clearly, they'd known each other for years, and they looked like they were having fun. I decided I want to join in, so I approached some of them, not really knowing what to do.

They didn't let me join them - they wouldn't let me play.

It hurt.

And that's when the masks started coming in.

Without even realising it, I started putting on masks.

I didn't know it at the time - indeed I didn't realise until decades later, but at some level in my unconscious I thought that if I could just pretend to be the sort of person they did like, then they'd let me play.

And so, the masks started appearing.

I was looking for anything that people might dislike about me, and then actively pretending that wasn't me, pretending I wasn't that person, pretending, in short, not to be me.

All in a bid to have them like me.

That formed a pattern which continued throughout my school life, throughout high school, and even into university life. Growing up in the 70s and 80s with no real role models, I would spend so much time and energy searching for, and finding, anything that people might dislike about me, so that I could hide it behind masks in the hopes they might get to like me.

Eventually I reached the age of about 25, and I got married. It was wonderful to start with. My wife and I really enjoying married life together.

Unfortunately, after the first year or so, things seemed to be going wrong. Married life wasn't quite the bed of roses, the everlasting bliss, that we had both assumed it would be. I was trying to work out what was going wrong, why was married life not working out for us?

And then one day it suddenly hit me.

A massive realisation, so obvious once it came, and yet one which was so deeply hidden until it reared its head.

Course my marriage wasn't working...

I'm gay!

You see, I had spent so much of my life hiding, so much of my life pretending to be somebody else, that I'd lost touch with who I was. In short, because of all my masks, I was effectively living a lie - I didn't even know who I was anymore...

I

INTRODUCING YOUR MASKS

1

WHAT IS A MASK?

If we are going to spend an entire book discussing masks, it makes sense that the first thing we should do is to define what we mean by masks - makes sense, right?

In this context, a mask is anything you are using to metaphorically hide part of who you are.

It could be pretending not to be who you are.

Or it could be pretending to be something you are not.

It might be not voicing your true feelings, or it might be denying your beliefs because you don't want others to know.

It could be saying what you think others want or expect you to say, or what you think you need to say to fit in; equally it might be NOT saying things, for the same reason.

It could be denying your heritage, making up a story about where you came from.

It could be pretending you don't like your favourite band because you might get ridiculed, or it could be pretending you do like a particular band so you "fit in" (even though you don't particularly care for their music).

It could be pretending that you are a successful business leader, because you are scared people would think less of you if they knew you had a part-time job to keep the bills paid while you build things up.

It might be never standing up for what you believe it, never countering arguments, never giving your true position in a discussion.

It could be pretending that a core part of your personality isn't there because you don't know of anyone else like that and you are scared you'll be judged or become an outcast for it.

How can you tell if you are wearing a mask?

The simplest way is to notice whether there are ever any situations or circumstances where you might hesitate to truthfully answer a question, or where you might hold back from saying or doing something, just because you fear others may judge you (or worse). If so, they you are undoubtedly wearing a mask in that situation.

It's also helpful to bear in mind that we don't just wear one mask - we will all be wearing layer upon layer of masks, and those masks may even change depending upon where we are and who we are with.

"What are you talking about? I'm not wearing any masks" you may well be thinking at this point.

Which would have been my exact reaction the day of my wedding had anyone suggested I was wearing a mask, and yet from the

Prologue we can see just how untrue that was. I was absolutely wearing a massive mask; I just didn't realise it.

It's true that most of us don't think we are wearing masks - and those are the most dangerous masks of all. The ones we have been wearing for so long, that we no longer even realise we are wearing them.

The good news is that by working your way through this book, you will start to become aware of those masks, and you will - if you so choose - find ways to remove them.

2

WHY DO WE WEAR MASKS?

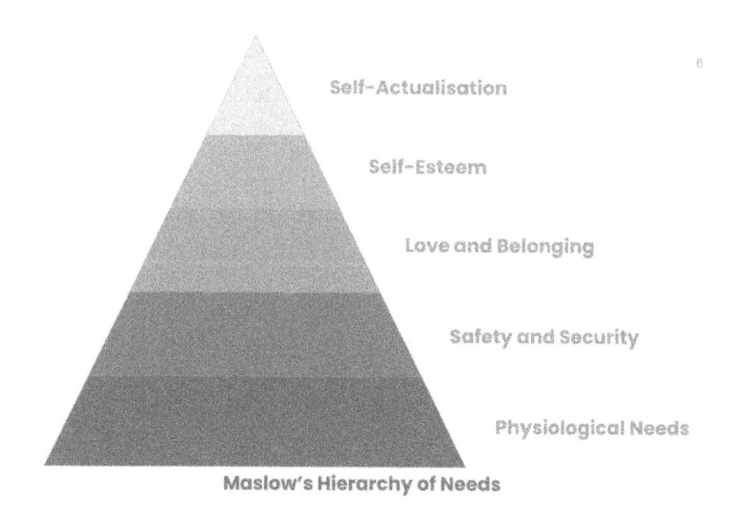

Maslow's Hierarchy of Needs

- Self-Actualisation
- Self-Esteem
- Love and Belonging
- Safety and Security
- Physiological Needs

Deep down, we all have a fundamental human need.

Well, we all have a lot of fundamental human needs, of course. The American psychologist Abraham Maslow first described these in 1943 in what has become known as Maslow's Hierarchy of Needs (if you want to explore this particular fascinating topic in more detail, you'd do well to start with Maslow's original article "A theory of human motivation" from 1943 which you can find in Psychological Review, 50(4), pages 370–396).

The main one which we are concerned with here, the one which generally results in the creation of masks, is that of belonging, and more specifically the need to be liked, or even to be loved.

In short, we all like to be liked - nobody likes to be disliked.

When I present this topic in a live talk, I'll illustrate the point by inviting the audience to "Put your hand up if you actually like to be disliked."

If it's a generally good-natured audience, especially one where many people know each other, then invariably at least one person will raise their hand. Naturally, this gets a nice laugh from the room.

"There's always one, isn't there?" I'll call out, in mock desperation, "and it's usually you!" to which they nod and smile, as more laughter sweeps the room.

Once everyone settles down again, I thank the hand-raiser for proving my point. Which is exactly what they have done. They proved, in a very immediate and memorable way, that nobody likes to be disliked.

The reason they raised their hand was because they knew they would get a laugh. And who doesn't enjoy it when they say or do something intentionally funny, to be rewarded with a nice laugh from the audience? They raised their hand because they knew it would get a laugh, which they knew they would enjoy getting, and which would make them feel warm for having entertained people however briefly and having gained a favourable reaction.

In short - they did it because they wanted people to like them.

Deep down, every single one of us likes to be liked.

It's a basic human need.

The reverse is also true - we don't like to be disliked. Nobody does. Not really, not deep down. Even those with the toughest of exteriors, deep down don't like being disliked, no matter how much they manage to hide that with their tough exterior.

The reality is, however, that throughout the entire history of humanity, absolutely nobody has been universally liked.

Nobody.

Even Christ, Buddha, the Prophet Mohammed, all had their detractors; they all had people who disliked or despised or even hated them.

Pick absolutely anyone, past or present, famous or not, and you will be able find people who dislike(d) them.

Indeed, think about the people who you personally admire or really like. Consider them carefully. Examine what you like about them, look at what you admire, really consider how massively positive an influence or role model they are for you. Then take a step back and realise that even here, there will be people out there who do not feel the same about this person - there will be people who dislike them, there will even be people who hate them for whatever reason.

Believe it or not, there are even people Out There who dislike me! I know, crazy, right? They'll be the ones reading this and thinking "Blimey, you think a lot of yourself…"

(I should add, as the written word is woefully inadequate for conveying humour, that this is of course a self-deprecating joke, and not a serious expression of my rampant ego. Mind you, there will be those who will view it as pure ego and as more proof that they are right to dislike me…)

The serious point though is that absolutely nobody has ever been liked by everyone. Everyone has their detractors, their haters, whatever you want to call it.

So of course, there are going to be those who dislike you. And you know what? That's OK! Because when you think about it, I bet there are people who you dislike. Of course there are. It's only natural.

But sometimes, the fear of the risk of being disliked can hurt so much that we are prepared to pretend we are not who we really are, to avoid risking someone disliking us.

So, we wear masks to pretend to be someone else, so that we'll be liked - we'll explore how well that works in a couple of chapters time.

At the start of this chapter I did say that the main Need which drives the wearing of masks is the need for love and belonging.

Which is true - that is the main reason we wear masks.

However, it would be remiss of us not to acknowledge that in some cases, there are situations where it is actually our perceived fear for our safety which causes us to wear certain masks. Indeed, in some situations, safety concerns are paramount, and hiding behind a mask may well feel like a prudent move. However, that is far rarer than most of us realise. Yes, in times of major conflict, self-preservation does require the wearing of multiple masks (both physical and metaphorical in some situations), but mercifully most of the time we are not in such situations.

3

WHERE DO THEY COME FROM?

Although the masks we wear in life can come from a number of places, and can develop in many different ways throughout life, there are typically a few common sources of them, which we'll take a look at in this chapter.

As we do, it is useful to remember that these are just examples of the most common causes of masks, and that it is possible for them to find other ways to sneak into our life. It's also worth noting that masks can (and often do) appear at any time in life - this is not just a childhood thing.

How, why, and where we develop our masks depends upon our stage in life. The concept of these stages of life is based upon work by the noted sociologist Dr Morris Massey, who described three main stages of development as we grow and become the human beings we currently are. Others have since added to his body of work, including describing a fourth stage and even stages beyond those.

In terms of usual causes of masks, we are most concerned with the first four stages, which we'll look at here.

The Imprint Period

This is generally from birth to around the age of seven. During this period, our mind is like a sponge - we absorb everything that is going on around us, and we accept it unquestioningly, especially when it comes from our parents. This stage of life has a tremendous impact on so many aspects of the rest of our life - we could discuss this in considerable depth (indeed when I teach NLP / Hypnosis / Coaching, we explore this a lot), but for our purposes here it is enough just to be aware than during our first seven or so years of life, we absorb everything unquestioningly. Through this we learn and adopt a lot of our life-skills, especially those related to dealing with our immediate environment. During this period, any masks we develop are very often going to be the same ones our parents have - we learn by absorbing what they do, and any behaviour caused by their masks will likewise start to imprint on us. We generally are unlikely to develop too many masks from this stage of our life, although it is not impossible by any means.

The Modelling Period

This is typically from around seven to around 13 or 14. Here we continue to copy our parents, but we now start to have an expanded circle of influence, and we will start to copy other people. Our period of blind acceptance is now behind us (partly due to the development of what is often known as the "Critical Faculty" - this is the part of our mind which is responsible for checking if things fit our beliefs and our preconceptions of the world). So rather than just accept everything we are told, we start to develop the ability to evaluate things for ourselves, like trying on a set of clothes to see if we like the way they look and feel on us. As I mentioned, we also now start to be more greatly influenced by people other than our parents. A particularly large influence is often our school teachers, although we might also be influenced by our youth group leaders, our church leaders, even our film / TV / music idols, resulting in us starting to adopt some of their particular views, beliefs, and even masks. Masks start to make more of an appearance here as we can start to feel we need to hide aspects of ourselves to please our parents or our main influencers.

The Socialisation Period

Between the ages of 13 or 14 to around 21, our primary circle of influence is our peers. As part of our developmental process we start to develop more of an individual identity, which very often causes us to look for ways to differentiate ourselves from our earlier influences. As a result, we will generally turn toward people who are more like "us", particularly our peers (which is why peer pressure can be such a massive influence, for good or bad, amongst teenagers). We also tend to find ourselves more greatly influenced by the media etc, especially those aspects which seem to fit with the values of our peer group. As one might imagine, this can be a huge source of masks. As part of learning from our peers, a great many of us feel pressured into conforming to the expectations and norms of our peer group. Which, for far too many, can mean we develop lots of masks to hide those aspects of us which don't conform, or those aspects of us which we fear our peer group will find distasteful. The fear of being "disowned" by one's peers, of being an outcast, is overwhelming enough that we will actively pretend not to be who we are, just so we can fit in. OR we may even find we feel we need to adopt masks to avoid or deflect bullying. This can be a massive problem for so many people in so many different ways. Effects which can last well beyond leaving school, alas.

The Business Persona

Although not a direct part of Dr Massey's work, many often describe the period where we develop what is known as our "business persona", which seems to be around the ages of 21 to 35. This corresponds for many to the period of our first "real" full time employment (especially those who go through higher education, although the same principles apply to us all). We are heavily influenced by our first work environment, our first work colleagues, our first boss. As we continue to find our place in the working environment, and continue to develop our careers, so this period continues to have a big influence upon us and our development. Again, this has a great many potential situations which can cause us to develop masks. The desire or even need to "fit in" with a work group can be even bigger than during our socialisation period. After all, here we risk not only ostracisation, we might even feel we risk our job or even career itself if we don't fit in. We may feel we have to be seen to be a particular "type" to have any chance at career progression. Or we may adopt various masks to avoid being the subject of 'Office Politics' or 'Office Gossip' (both insidious things). This can also happen outside of the work place as we seek to find our identity in the bigger outside world - and let's face it, no matter how well-prepared we may have been throughout our childhood and adolescent years, nothing can truly fully prepare us for this stage of life. Is it any wonder therefore that so many of us end up developing masks?

There are other stages of our life, of course (such as "Midlife", typically from 36 - 50, where we can start to question our identity as well as starting to become increasingly aware of our own mortality), and all of these will have an influence on our development of masks. However, the initial four periods are perhaps the most significant in terms of us developing and wearing masks, especially the ones we wear without even being aware of them.

Part of the problem with masks is that once we start wearing them, we feel trapped. Even if we are aware of the masks, we feel we can never remove them because the pressures which caused us to wear them are still there.

Worse, even if those initial pressures go away, we still often feel unable to remove our masks, because how can we suddenly change who we are in front of all those people who have got to know us this way?

4

WHAT HAPPENS WHEN WE WEAR A MASK?

Are masks that bad? What is the problem with wearing masks, if they help us be more liked and keep us safe?

If that's what masks did, then that would probably be fine.

Unfortunately, the reality is very different, and masks are harmful - sometimes very harmful.

Let's look at what happens when we wear masks. It turns out that there are a couple of main things for us to notice here.

You'll remember from earlier in this book we noted that the main reason people wear masks is that they are afraid that they might be disliked, and we wear a mask to hide that aspect of us.

Does this mean that "they" won't dislike us?

To start with, yes. When we wear a mask, when we hide those aspects, when we pretend not to be who we are, the mask may indeed successfully hide that part of us away from people. And sure enough, we find that the people who we'd feared might not otherwise like us, don't run away from us. They don't see that thing which they would dislike, so they don't block us. Indeed, over time we might even actually start to form some sort of relationship with them: personal, professional or whatever.

However, there is still a massive danger.

You see, the more we develop any form of relationship with them, the greater the risk that inevitably at some point cracks will start to appear in the mask. Or that the mask will, however, fleetingly slip. Either way they will catch a glimpse of who is behind the mask.

When they do that, the thing which they were hiding away becomes visible; they will get to see it, even if it's just momentarily, they will get to see it.

Now, if that is something which, as we feared, they would have disliked then they can see it and they now start to dislike us because we are the very thing that we knew they wouldn't like.

But it's worse than that.

You see, just because people dislike something, it doesn't mean they would automatically dislike a person for it. There might be reasons they may have made allowances. For example, I suspect many of us can think of couples who have very different political views, differences which could otherwise result in heated arguments, and yet the couple are clearly devoted to each other because they recognise that one difference is not that big a deal.

Unfortunately, in this case by hiding that part of us away, we have in effect been lying to that other person. We've been deceiving them, even making a fool of them (in their eyes).

If there's one thing people really hate, it's when you make a fool of them.

So of course, now they are going to dislike you because of that thing that they dislike *and* they're going to dislike you even more because you have been lying to them and making a fool of them.

Plus, it's not done any good for your reputation within that group of people, as others then find out you were misleading them.

So rather than protect us from possible dislike, all the mask has ultimately done is made them dislike us even more strongly than they otherwise might have done.

As if that were not enough, what about the other side of the coin?

Consider that whatever aspect you are fearful of revealing, there are people in the world who would like you for it. There are people who will need you for what you stand for. There will be people who would be inspired by knowing you think or feel that way. They like doing the things you like doing. They have the same belief that you that you believe in. Those people could have become acquaintances, friends, you could have formed strong relationships with them. However, because you are hiding behind the mask, they don't get to see any of that. So, they don't get to connect to you.

It would be like having a shop which is filled with beautiful, wondrous things that people really need love, need, and could benefit from.

But.

You make sure the shop has no name, you ensure there is no description, and you absolutely ensure that you do not advertise anywhere.

All the windows are boarded up so nobody can see inside.

Even the doors are closed, locked off.

And you hide the shop down a side alley.

How many people are going to come into that shop and see for themselves what's in there?

Nobody.

Everyone is going to walk on past to the other shops - shops which are displaying their wares in the window for all to see, so that people can make a decision. If people don't like what they see they'll simply carry on past.

On the other hand, if they do like what they see, then they'll pop in and take a closer look.

But they are absolutely not going to be visiting your hidden, closed off, unappealing shop.

It's the same when we wear masks. You do not give people a chance to get to know you. You give them no reason to want to get to know you because they see nothing in common.

A basic aspect of a rapport, which is a key part in all successful human interactions, is that we tend to like people who are like us. So, when you hide behind a mask, you hide all those things that people might get to like you for. Which means you are denying them the chance to connect with you. So, they just carry on past.

And all of that makes for a very lonely life, because now you've got the people who you were afraid would dislike you disliking you anyway, which they were always going to do, *and* you're preventing people who might have liked you from getting a chance to like you.

It's a very lonely place to be indeed.

That's the dual risks of wearing masks; it backfires in so many ways.

Ultimately, although we feel that the mask will protect us, it's quite the reverse.

5

WHAT HAPPENS WHEN WE TAKE IT OFF?

So, what happens when we take the masks off?

It turns out that there are three main things which are worth our attention.

Let's start off by looking at the people who we are afraid will dislike us. Remember, this is the primary reason we tend to wear masks, so that we don't give them a reason to dislike us.

Yes, when we remove our mask, they will see that particular aspect which we were hiding. And yes, they may dislike us for it as a result. There is no question about that, no way to avoid it, it happens.

Remember, however, that as we've already seen, nobody in the entire history of humanity has ever been universally liked. Christ, Buddha, Prophet Mohammed, all had their detractors.

Did they go around pleading "Why don't you like me?"

Did they go round begging and pleading to be liked?

Of course not!

Heck, if they did do that they would just give the people who disliked them an even bigger reason to dislike them. "Oh, keep away from them, they are just a whiny so-and-so".

Not only that, but the people who might have got to like the things that they think, say, or do, get put off as well because nobody likes a person who's constantly whining.

When Christ, Buddha, the Prophet Mohammed, had all these people who disliked them, they simply acknowledged that those people didn't like them, they accepted it, and they then got on with the infinitely more important task of sharing their message of love, sharing it far and wide with those who needed to hear it, sharing it with those who liked them, and with those who had yet to form any opinion either way.

They made sure that what they were offering was openly on display in the shop window. People could see and decide for themselves and those who liked it came in. They focused their attention on those who did like them, all those who had yet to form an opinion.

So, yes, when we remove our masks, there will be people who dislike us.

And that's OK.

Because it's not actually personal.

Wait, what? How can it not be personal? "It's me they dislike, it doesn't get any more personal than that Keith, what are you on about?"

When you think about it, and I mean take a step back and really think about it for a moment, it's not actually you that they dislike.

After all, how can it be? They haven't had a chance to get to know you yet.

So no, it's not you they dislike.

It's not even the thing you thought or said or did that they dislike.

And it's not even their impression of what they think you thought or said or did that they dislike.

What they dislike is their interpretation of their perception of their impression of what they think you thought or said or did.

It's not actually about you at all.

It's all about their feelings, emotions, prejudices, beliefs, attitudes, situation, environment... all these factors which relate to them and not you.

It's absolutely nothing about you at all, it's really all about them.

It's as impersonal as it's possible to get.

I get it, I know it can feel personal when people dislike you, but it's never really you they are disliking.

We are all more than one thing. We are all complex individuals. When people dislike someone because they say a particular thing, they are ignoring absolutely everything else that person stands for and is. And the reason those people don't even think about that is because they've never had a chance to connect with that person because they have ruled out any possibility of connecting that person, because they dislike their interpretation of their perception of their impression of what they think that you thought, said, or did.

It's never you personally that dislike.

So, yes, when we remove the masks, people will dislike us. And that is absolutely fine. Think about it. You don't like everybody. There are people who you dislike, right? That's just part of human nature.

So that's the people who might dislike you, what about the people who might like you? What about the people who might like what we stand for, what we think, say, or do?

When we remove our masks, when we stand there without the masks, being who we are, people can see us for who we are.

There will be many people who like what we say, people who need to hear what we say, people who will look to us for support in what we say. And because we are not hiding behind our masks, those people get to see us for who we truly are, and they get a chance to connect with us. Remember we said about rapport? We tend to like those who are like us. They will see things in you which they like, which are similar to them. And they will connect with you.

Now, I'm not saying it's going to happen instantly. Of course it won't. But over time, people will be drawn to you. And they'll get to know you. And the more they get to know about you, the more they can decide "Actually, I kind of like this person. I like hanging out with them because we think the same things."

By removing your mask, you start to attract to you those people who like what you think, say, and do. You also attract those who *need* what you think, say, or do.

That's what happens when you remove your masks. You start to attract the company of those who are like you. And let's face it, isn't that a lot better to be liked for what you are, than to be liked for who you are not?

It's a lot less exhausting, for one thing. Never having to pretend.

So, people get to like you for who you are. You attract and build your following, your tribe, your circle - whatever you want to call it. Your circle becomes filled with people who have similar thoughts, dreams, ambitions and beliefs to you.

And that is a beautiful place to be.

Your vibe attracts your tribe. As a saying goes, that's exactly what happens here. You attract to you people who resonate with what you stand for. It's a beautiful place to be, because not only do you develop a lot of relationships and friendships, but by coming together you can create something wonderful, something powerful, something greater than the sum of all of you.

You can create a movement.

There is also a third thing which happens as a direct result of you removing your masks.

When you stand there for who you are, allowing the world to see who you are, hear what you say, understand what you believe in, to see what you do - when you remove your masks, you give other people permission to be who *they* are. You can serve as a guide and inspiration, or even as a role model, for countless other people. Both for those around you, and for those with whom may never actually come into direct contact.

People who get to realise that they are not the only one who thinks that way, or believes those beliefs, or wants to do those things.

They get to realise that there are others (such as you) who are like them.

By you being you, you show them that it's OK to be who they are. You give them permission to be themselves.

You let them see that they do not have to spend their lives cowering behind masks.

Also, you might inspire some other people to stand for who they are.

Which, in turn, will enable them to serve as an inspiration for others beyond, and so on and so on. This creates an amazing ripple effect - when you throw a stone into a pond, the ripples spread out way beyond the point the stone hit. Similarly, the effect of you standing there being you and empowering and inspiring others to be themselves, creates a ripple which spreads out far beyond your circle, impacting and empowering others who may never have even heard of you, but who have been empowered indirectly.

All because you removed your masks and showed the world it's OK to be you.

Isn't that a wonderful gift to be able to give other people? To give them the ability to know that they can be who they are, to reassure them that it's okay to be who they are.

All that happens because you've removed your mask.

II

RELEASING YOUR MASKS

6

HOW DO WE TAKE THEM OFF?

So far, we have looked at what masks are and where they come from, examined why we wear masks, and we've explored the harm which these masks cause - both for us and for others. We have also started to look at what life can be like for us once we remove those masks. We've seen that yes, removing our masks does mean that some people might dislike us, but we are now in a much better place because we know that it's OK to be disliked, and we can now actually see and understand that it's never actually personal - we know that it's not actually us they dislike.

We have also started to see the wonderful opportunities and powerful way-of-life which opens up for us once we do remove our masks, and the amazing way in which that helps not only us and those around us, but can (and does) actually help countless people around the world, people who we will never even meet or know about, but who we inspire by being our mask-free selves.

All of which will most likely have given rise to the realisation that the best way for us to live a rich and fulfilling life is to show ourselves, to destroy our fears, and to release our masks.

Which just leaves the question of how?

How DO we remove our masks?

The good news is that you have already taken what is probably the hardest step of all - becoming aware that masks actually exist, and becoming aware that you are wearing masks, and open to the possibility that they can be removed.

This really is good news because it puts you well ahead of perhaps the majority of the population who carry on blissfully unaware that they are wearing masks, blissfully unaware of the damage they are causing, and even oblivious to the fact that masks even exist.

Just before we dive into how we can remove them; it is very useful to take a moment or two first to pause and really consider why we want to remove them.

"You've just said we need to remove our masks, and now you are asking me why? What's going on Keith?"

A good question, dear reader, and one which deserves an answer of course.

You see, at this stage you we could rush headfirst into looking at how to remove the masks, and you would get some small results from that, of course.

However, if we spend a little time on this step first then the results we will get when we *do* start looking at how to remove our masks will be much bigger and better.

HOW DO WE TAKE THEM OFF? | 39

For now, turn your attention to why you want to remove those masks - and right now it's OK to not know what some, or even any, of those masks are. Right now, you just know that you want to remove them, whatever they may be.

The question right now is why?

You may wish to set aside an hour or so where you can be completely undisturbed for this bit, you get far better results when you do it all in one single go rather than coming back to it. However, it is also important that you do it, so make sure you aren't using the "I haven't got a spare hour" as an excuse to skip it.

Remember - if this is important to you (and it is important to you isn't it? Otherwise you would not be reading this, would you?), then you will find a way to find that hour now.

You are also going to need (at least) a couple of fresh sheets of paper and a pen - it is far more effective to do this by hand the old fashioned way with pen and paper, than to type it on your computer or tablet.

On the top of one sheet write "How masks are holding me back", and at the top of the second sheet write "How removing masks frees me". Then spend some time in quiet contemplation, writing down all the answers which come to mind for you on both points.

Remember, at this stage it doesn't matter whether you know what the masks are or not, that will come later.

Right now, all you need to focus on are all the areas in which not being your true self is harming you, actively holding you back; and all the things which allowing yourself to be your true self will enable you to achieve - the hopes, dreams, ambitions it enables you to fulfil, and all the other wonderful effects which your being you will have for you, those around you, and the world in general.

Think small level and think big level - for this covers the entire range of experiences.

Remember to accept whatever suggestions come up - for they are all coming from your own unconscious mind. Accept each suggestion, thank your mind for sharing them with you, and ask it if it would like to share more. Eventually you will reach the point where you cannot think of anymore. You are not done yet - far from it, you are now about to hit the really interesting part. Again thank your mind for bringing you all these amazing answers, perhaps look over them, and then ask yourself if there were any other answers, what might they be? And just relax your mind, allowing whatever wants to come up to do so. Sometimes they will come quickly, sometimes they may take a few moments of hesitation before they venture to suggest themselves. Either way, be relaxed, patient, and accepting of whatever comes up.

Again, sooner or later you will feel your mind draws a blank. Again, thank it for everything, and encourage it to consider if there were any more answers, what might they be? And relax, allowing whatever happens to happen. Do not attempt to force anything, just sit and relax and allow thoughts to come and go as they wish, until eventually more answers come.

Eventually, for a third time, you will hit a blank - you can now consider that you really have got everything down, and you can stop waiting for answers.

At this stage, it is time to take a look back over both sheets of paper, examining and exploring each answer you've uncovered, and for each one, spend some time pondering why that is important to you. You may even find it helpful to take another sheet of paper and to start writing down some of the new answers which come to you.

For example, look at your "How masks are holding me back" sheet and take the first thing you wrote there. Ask yourself why that thing would be important to you, and why masks holding you back is so bad for you. Really examine everything which comes up. Keep going through all the answers you wrote on that sheet.

Then move to the "How removing masks frees me" sheet. Take each statement you wrote on there in turn, and ask yourself why is the thing important to you? What does it get for you? Why is that important to you and your family? What benefit would you gain? Again, really consider all the possibilities before you move on to the next answer on that sheet and repeat the process until you have got through them all.

Once you have finished this exercise, you might want to take a little break - perhaps go get some fresh air or have a glass of water, just let your mind chill out for a few moments before diving into the next section, just as you might take a short break if you'd been doing some particularly strenuous workout at the gym. Your mind has been working out significantly, and there are more demands to be placed upon it in the next couple of chapters, so take a metaphorical breather for a few minutes and then we'll continue - you are just getting started, and that's something to be excited about.

7

A SIMPLE QUESTION

By now you are not only ready to start removing your masks, if you have done the previous exercise fully then you are probably almost chomping at the bit to remove them. Which is a great place from which to start the next step of the process.

The next step on our journey of mask removal is to ask ourselves a very simple question.

When we ask ourselves this question, and truly allow ourselves the time and space we need to really get to grips with the answer, then we are well on the way to removing our masks.

By asking ourselves this question, we start to allow the masks to slip, to crack, and we start to get glimpses of the person underneath them all - the person who is actually us.

Sometimes when people consider this question, they get an almost lightbulb moment, a great "Aha!" revelation as clarity suddenly snaps into focus and the masks tumble away.

If that happens for you – fantastic.

If, on the other hand, that doesn't happen for you, then that's all good too - it just means you are in the majority, the people for whom the answers will come in their own good time, just not immediately.

So, when you ask yourself this question, don't worry if you don't feel like you have suddenly achieved Nirvana - different people will react differently, and will get different results, and that's all good. We are, after all, all different people with different experiences, so naturally our results will be different.

And so, to the question itself. It is a very simple question.

"Who was I before society told me who I should be?"

I said it was a simple question - I didn't say it was going to be easy to answer. After all, it has taken you pretty much your entire life to reach this point, to develop all the masks you are wearing - so it's OK if it takes you a little while to figure them all out.

"Who was I before society told me who I should be?"

That person is the real you, free from all the masks you've been wearing. That is the person the world needs to see. That is the person you truly deserve to be, to celebrate, to nurture.

"Who was I before society told me who I should be?"

It is a question which can be explored in a great many ways, and whose answers can come to us in many forms.

What follows are a few different ways in which people have found it helpful when asking themselves the question, these are presented in the hope that you might find one or more of them useful yourself, or that they inspire some other ideas which may work even more powerfully for you. Remember, there is no right or wrong, there is no one-size-fits-all. Whatever works for you is exactly the right approach for you. It doesn't matter how others do it, you do it your way.

- Meditation. If you practise any form of meditation, then a great way to consider the question is to meditate upon it. Set it as your focus for one or more sessions. Read and remind yourself of the question before you start, asking your mind to ponder the possible answers, then go with the flow and relax into whatever comes up.
- Journalling. If you have a journalling practise, it can be very interesting to set yourself the challenge of journalling on that theme from time to time. Write the question at the start of your journalling period, and then just write, in stream-of-consciousness format, everything which comes out. No judgements, no evaluation, just constantly write and write and write until there is no more. Then examine what has come up, look for hints, clues, answers, patterns. Some people find it helpful to do this as a regular practise, at least to start with.
- Before going to sleep. As you are settling down to sleep, ask yourself the question. Perhaps repeat it to yourself a few times, even using it as a mantra while you fall asleep. Ask your unconscious mind to fully explore the question and to offer you answers in whatever way feels right, then be open to whatever comes up. It might give you interesting dreams, or you might find your head fills with

answers as you wake up. It can be helpful to have a notepad and pen by your bed so that you can write down whatever comes to you as soon as you wake up. Don't wait until you've got up and dressed etc before planning to write them down, you know how quickly those thoughts first thing in the morning can disappear forever.
- Ponder it. Perhaps during a nice quiet walk in the countryside, or whilst enjoying a well-deserved leisurely soak in the bath, just ponder the question. Mull it over in your mind, and then just relax and open your mind up to allowing whatever comes up to come up.

These are some of the ways people have found helpful in answering the question. There are, of course, countless other ways to do it, and different ones will work for different people. Just go with whatever feels right for you.

"Who was I before society told me who I should be?"

Be open to asking yourself that question many times over the coming days, weeks, even months. The chances are there will be a lot more answers than you first uncover. Remember, it has taken you a lifetime to build these masks up, it's OK if it takes you some time to uncover the answers.

8

GOING DEEPER

By now you should have started to catch a glimpse of who is lurking under all those masks.

Hopefully, you might even have started to reconnect with that person, to get back in touch with their hopes and fears, their dreams, and ambitions, their beliefs, and aspirations.

It's now time for us to dig even deeper into finding out who exactly is underneath all those masks, by turning our attention to the masks themselves. Remember that the mere fact of becoming aware of a mask makes it so much easier to remove the mask. Very often the mask itself will start to crack and melt and fall away just because of the spotlight of attention being turned upon it.

There are a few different ways in which we can go deeper in our exploration of the masks we wear. Each one helps us to gain a deeper understanding of who we truly are, so even if we were not looking to remove our masks, each one of these is a very useful and interesting process to go through in its own right.

48 | THE MASKS WE WEAR

Some people find they prefer to pick only one and stick with that, and they will indeed get results. I would strongly recommend that you look at all of them and do all of the processes (although not all at the same time, that would just be chaos).

WHERE YOU HIDE

As we explored the question of why we wear masks in the first part of this book, we came to understand that a major factor is that there are things we wish to hide from others, for whatever reason. (I say, "for whatever reason", of course we both know the reasons ultimately boil down to "they might not like me for this".)

Which means we can get a lot of insight into our masks by taking a good look at where in life we are hiding.

That hiding can take many forms, and we'll explore some of those here. You are encouraged to continue exploring and to see what other forms you have been unwittingly adopting until now.

- Avoiding places or events or people
- Avoiding saying things
- Pretending not to have certain beliefs
- Never daring to voice your opinion

You might be like Doug, for example, who really loved a particular band. He'd always liked their music, the songs really spoke to him, he was quite a fan. He had all their material. However, Doug felt that he could not talk about his love for this band - not with his friends, who he feared would ridicule or judge him (or worse) for his musical tastes, and not with his work colleagues for similar reasons. When he gave lifts in his car, he had to make sure none of his band's music was there. When he had friends round, he made sure the band's CDs were hidden away. He never got round to seeing his band play on any of their tours, partly in case anyone spotted him, and partly because he had nobody to go along with. Eventually his band released their final album and played their final gig and Dough had never had the chance to see them, nor to share his passion for their music with anyone…

Or you might be like Jane. Jane has some strong views and beliefs about life and how we all treat each other, but Jane was always wary of speaking up in case she got judged or criticised. So, she would always keep her views to herself, never speaking up when things happened which conflicted with them. Never standing up for those who needed her support. Over time, this all just ate away at her. She started to feel more and more powerless, felt more enraged by the injustices which she felt powerless to do anything about. Which made her feel angry, upset, and really started to affect her over time. All of which inevitably impacted upon her health, her relationships, her interactions with others - the strain of hiding away really took its toll.

Perhaps you might be like Jeff. Jeff had dreams, ambitions, and a strong view of what he wanted to be when he grew up. Sadly, those around him didn't support those views. They felt he was misguided at best and wasted no opportunity to ridicule him, to undermine him, and to generally make his ambitions the butt of their jokes. So over time, Jeff moved away from pursuing his dreams, he settled for a normal career path, doing what others thought he should be doing. He did OK, made reasonable money, but felt increasingly devoid of joy. His career was draining, held no real passion for him, and life became dull as a result as his old passion was smothered and allowed to wither away unfulfilled…

WHAT DID YOU LOVE DOING?

This can be a very powerful one indeed! What did you love doing, that you no longer do?

This be related to the question from the previous chapter, but this goes so much deeper.

Interestingly, not only does this question help you to get an even deeper insight into your masks, especially the ones you've been wearing for a *really* long time; this can also help to rekindle old, long-lost ambitions, desires, hobbies, and interests. You never know what you are going to find, and what you will end up rediscovering as a result here. Indeed, so powerful is this aspect that we will revisit it in more detail later in the book.

But for now, it's time for us to go on a journey of discovery, a journey back into your past and at the same time deep into your soul.

Take some time and space to allow yourself to quietly contemplate, in whatever way feels right for you.

For example, if you practise meditation of any form, then this would form a great basis for a meditation - meditate on your younger self, on getting in touch with the younger you who is still very much deep inside of you, connect with your younger self, and explore what they/you loved doing, what lights you both up.

On the other hand, if meditation is not your thing, that's perfectly OK too. Instead, simply find some time to be able to sit quietly, where you won't be disturbed for a period of time. Allow your eyes to close as you relax and start to remember what it was like to be a young you. If you find it difficult to remember, then just imagine what it might have been like - you'll be surprised just how much detail your unconscious mind will happily fill in to make the imagination complete.

Either way, notice what you notice. Don't force anything, and don't judge anything. Just allow whatever wants to come up to do so, and notice what you notice.

What did this younger you really enjoy doing that you now no longer do? How did they pass their time? Things which you don't do any more for whatever reason? At this stage it is important not to judge or seek to explain, just allow everything that wants to come up to do so.

Get really curious about what you are uncovering.

As you do so, also examine whether there were things the young you liked but felt they had to hide from others. What feelings, thoughts, wishes, beliefs did they have that you no longer have? And what feelings, thoughts, wishes, beliefs, hopes and dreams did they have but which they felt they could not share with others, but instead had to hide for whatever reason.

As you go through this, you might find you feel some pangs of sorry or regret for dreams long lost. It's OK. It's OK to feel sad for them and as you do, realise that they are not lost forever - indeed, later in the book we'll see that what you are doing now can give them a very real opportunity to be rekindled.

Right now, however, just be aware of whatever comes up.

Because each of these things which do surface are pointers and hints to the masks you have been wearing in life. Each one of these memories is important, because they increase awareness of your specific masks.

You see, when we are aware of a particular mask, wearing that mask has now suddenly become a choice rather than an unshakable necessity.

And because wearing that mask is a choice now, you are free to be able to choose to remove that mask. When you choose to be able to remove a mask, that means that you must remove it; and when you must remove it, that means that you can remove it, which in turn means that you will remove it.

It all starts with awareness - the "how" we will discover in the next chapters, for now focus on developing the awareness of those masks.

9

DEALING WITH THE FEAR

As we saw earlier on, fear plays a big part in why we wear masks. Which means it should come as no surprise to find that when faced with the decision to remove our masks, we can face a lot of fear. Sometimes that fear can be enough to stop us from removing those masks, causing us to shrink back into our old life, hiding away from the world.

There is, however, one very important thing to realise about fear.

Fear is nothing to be scared of.

At first glance, this sounds ridiculous. Of course, fear is scary. It is fear, after all.

However, we truly do not have to be afraid of fear. Indeed, as we shall shortly start to realise, fear can be our friend; it can be a very helpful ally when facing the world.

To help us understand this a little more clearly, let's go for a ride in the car.

Imagine the scene - you are driving along. Perhaps you are heading on an exciting adventure, or perhaps you are visiting friends, or maybe it is a more mundane trip to work or the shops. It doesn't really matter, what does matter is that you are in the driver's seat, happily driving the car, everything under control.

And then suddenly, unexpectedly, unannounced, and seemingly out of nowhere, a light suddenly lights up on the dashboard.

There's no mistaking it - a bright red light, shining out at you from the dashboard. It wasn't there a moment ago, and now it is demanding attention.

At this point, you have three different options which are available to you.

1. You could react in terror, screaming, leaping out of the car and, assuming you miraculously escape without injury, run away as far and as fast as you can, never looking back, never going anywhere near that (or any other) car ever again. It would be seen by many as perhaps a slightly extreme over-reaction, but it is certainly an option which is open to you.
2. You could ignore the light, hoping that it will go away. Keep on driving on your journey convinced that the light is unimportant, that you can ignore it, and that it will eventually just disappear back from whence it emerged. Of course, you and I both know that this light is not going anywhere. It is going to remain resolutely lit, because the fault which has caused the light to illuminate is not going to go away. The longer you leave it, the longer you ignore

it, the worse the fault will get. Until it reaches a catastrophic failure which, depending upon the location of the fault, could means a very expensive repair bill - if, indeed, the car can be repaired at all. Worst case, the fault is such that continuing to use the car is dangerous, risking life and limb - such as a warning that the brake system has failed.

3. You could recognise it for what it is - a warning light alerting you to the fact that something needs your attention. You could then pay attention to the warning the light is giving you. Note what it is telling you, and decide whether this is something which demands immediate attention, in which case you pull to the side of the road and deal with it; or whether this can wait until you get home or you can get to a garage to deal with it. If you know how to resolve the problem, then you can resolve it as quickly as possible, to minimise the risk of damage to the car. If you don't know how to resolve it, then you simply take it to an expert who can help you, such as your friendly local mechanic who is an expert on this make and model of car, and who quickly brings their considerable skills to tackle the problem and to get your car back to full working order.

Faced with the warning light and with these three options, which one will you decide to follow?

It's a pretty safe bet to assume you are not going to go with option 1, no matter what the warning light is.

As tempting as option 2 may be (and let's face it, we probably both know of people who do tend to go for option 2, and then wonder why their car breaks down and costs a fortune to fix), if we are rational and logical about things, we can safely dismiss this option as being viable.

Which leaves us with option 3.

We check the information the warning light is giving us, and make a quick decision - does this need immediate attention (such as brake failure, or engine oil has run out, or the engine is overheating), does this require attention very soon but not immediately (such as perhaps the fuel warning light coming on, letting us know we have maybe 30 miles until we run out of fuel), or is this something which means that we can safely complete our journey, provided we then attend to the underlying fault as soon as is practical (such as the Service Due light coming on).

Then, once we know how serious and urgent the issue is, we can give it our attention accordingly. When it comes to resolving the issue, if we know enough about it we can do that ourselves (be that refuelling, or checking and topping up the coolant, or even servicing the car if we are so equipped and inclined). On the other hand, if it is something beyond our current knowledge and skills, then we rely upon a trusted expert, such as our friendly local car mechanic who we know from experience will do a good job for us at a reasonable price.

So, what happened here?

You were driving, the car warned you that something needed your attention, you assessed how urgent the warning was, and then you resolved the underlying problem in a timely fashion.

The warning light simply meant that something needed attention.

Of course, if there was only one single light on the entire dashboard, that could make things a little trickier.

Fortunately, there are various different warning lights in a car, making it a little easier to figure out what is wrong, how urgent it is, and how to fix it - one light warns your indicators are on, another warns you are not wearing a seatbelt, yet another warns that you are low on fuel, and so on.

So, it is with fear.

Fear is nothing more than your unconscious mind giving you a signal to alert you that something needs attention.

That it all fear is - a warning light to say, "Excuse me, this needs some attention".

Sadly, so many of us always take option 1 whenever any fear arises - we panic, bail out, get as far away as we can, and resolve never to get close to that situation ever again.

However, when we train ourselves to recognise that fear is nothing more than a sign that something needs a little attention, we can start to pause, to listen to our unconscious, to check what that inner voice is alerting us to, and we can take the time to discover what specifically it is which needs our attention.

At which point, we can decide how urgently we need to address it, and then we can address it in a timely manner. Either solving it ourselves, or seeking help - which might be from a partner, or from friends, or colleagues, or peers, or an expert in that particular area.

They key is to take the time to really listen to what your unconscious is attempting to tell you. Pay attention to your intuition, listen to your gut, however you want to describe the process.

For someone who is not used to doing this, it sounds daunting, verging on impossible. However, it absolutely is possible, and what's more, anyone can develop this skill - it just takes practise.

Next time you are scared, or you notice you are feeling fear, try the following and see what happens.

1. Acknowledge the fear. Acknowledge that there is fear, which means there is something to which you need to pay attention.
2. Thank your unconscious for alerting you and bringing it to your attention. Sounds a bit weird, but don't worry, it can be as simple as just saying a silent "Thank you".
3. Get curious as to what, specifically, needs the attention. Is there something you have overlooked, for example? Just allow whatever comes up to come up, trust your unconscious or your instinct or your intuition or your gut or whatever you feel is appropriate to call it.
4. Once you realise what needs attention, what you've missed, you can start to solve it.

I'm not saying it will necessarily be easy, especially when you start, but as with most things, the more you practise this, the easier it will get, and the better you will get at recognising the signs earlier and of solving the issues sooner.

Of course, there are some fears where the cause is obvious and very immediate - if that's the case, don't spend time meditating and contemplating, just do whatever is needed right away.

Over time, as you practise this more and more, you will start to notice the early warning signs. Such as that little niggling feeling at the back of your mind, for example. And you can use these to solve the problem long before it becomes a problem.

What does all of this have to do with our masks, you may be thinking by this point?

Again, remember that generally we wear masks as a form of protection, driven by fear. Usually the fear that people will dislike us or judge us, although sometimes other fears can have the same result.

Being aware the masks are driven by fear, we can now be more aware - when we feel we are in a situation where we might be very tempted to wear a mask, we can now acknowledge the fear and look to resolve the underlying issue, rather than just hide behind yet another mask.

Now, of course, even knowing all of this, there are some people who will still find it really difficult to let go of their fears, people who will find it difficult to embrace their fears and use them to create a more enjoyable life.

Why is this?

It usually boils down to one of five main reasons, which we will touch on briefly now.

1 They Are A Great Excuse

Sounds harsh, but for many people, their fear can be a very good excuse for all manner of things.

Especially it can be a great excuse for failure.

I've known of many people who use their fear or their phobia as a justification for pretty much anything that goes wrong, and as a cast-iron excuse for failing in something, without accepting any of the responsibility.

Of course, the reality is that the fear is very rarely the actual cause of the problem. Usually they fail for other reasons – not working hard enough at it, giving up too early, not focusing on the problem, not working through it methodically, not knowing what to do, not willing to do whatever it takes, the list goes on.

However, instead of recognising those and taking responsibility and doing something, many find it far easier to blame it on their fear.

After all, it's not their fault, it's the fear's fault, so they can hardly be to blame when it all goes wrong...

So, if they were to address their fear, to conquer it once and for all – well, there goes their excuse.

2 It's Comfortable.

As absurd as it may sound at first, for some people fear can be a very comfortable and even reassuring thing.

Sure, it stops them from doing many things, but hey, some of those things are quite scary, you know?

On the other hand, when we are living with the fear, or living with the phobia, it does provide us with some degree of comfort. This is because you know exactly and almost instinctively how you are going to react in any given situation, you know what will happen, you know what to expect.

It's comfortable. The very definition of living within the comfort zone.

Alas, much of the good stuff (including very often the way to get our dreams) lies outside of the comfort zone, and as much of a comfort blanket as our fear may be, it is still ultimately holding us back.

But hey, at least it's comfortable there.

3 "It's Part Of Who I Am"

A *very* common comment people with fears or phobias make is "It's just part of who I am".

In this case, people have chosen to embrace their fears as part of their personality, and as a core part of who they are.

Which is a massive shame, because the reality is that none of us are born with fears. None of us are born scared of anything. We are born completely fearless (as countless parents of young babies will attest from their own nerve-wracking experiences with their fearless offspring).

All fears are things we learn to do – either through direct experience or by observing others or through being taught.

Which means that no matter what the fear is, it is categorically not a part of who we are. It is simply something we learned to do along the way.

And of course, if we learned how to do the fear, we can also learn how NOT to do the fear. Indeed, that's probably the main work I do with my coaching clients, helping them to learn how not to do the fear and how to react in positive, helpful, empowering ways instead. It's how I conquered my own three phobias in the past, too, so I know it is entirely possible.

4 You Are Scared Of Life Without Them

Life can be scary at times.

For anyone.

And one of the biggest sources of scariness can be the worry of the unknown. When you know what it going to happen, when you know how to react, it is less scary. On the other hand, if you are not sure what is going to happen, then you can't plan how to react, and that makes it scary.

So, for people who have fears which hold them back from doing new things, the fear itself can be reassuring.

How?

While you have the fear, it stops you from trying new things. So, you remain where you are, which means you know how to act.

On the other hand, if you get rid of your fear, and have no excuse but to Do The Thing, then you end up in a new situation, uncharted territory, complete with a new set of challenges – you enter the (partially) unknown.

And for many people, the thought of that can be even scarier, so they cling on to their current fear as an excuse not to do something new.

5 You Just Don't Think It's Possible To Change

Many people I've spoken to about their fear or phobia have expressed the belief that it is impossible for them to change, to get rid of it.

The reality is that we are constantly changing – we are not the same today as we were yesterday. Indeed, look back at you from ten years ago, see just how much has changed in your views, your beliefs, your situation, your attitudes, your knowledge…

We are constantly changing – sometimes in big way, more usually in small subtle ways. But changing we are.

You were not born with your fear, you learned it – in other words, you changed from being fearless to being scared.

So of course, with the right guidance and direction, you can absolutely change and conquer your fear. After all, since 2010 I've helped over 5,000 people (including myself) in five continents to transform their deepest fears into their greatest strengths, and provided you are prepared to let go of your fear, you too can change and experience the wondrous new possibilities which open up as a result.

10

RETURN OF THE MASK?

By now, if you have been working along with the exercises whilst reading this book, you will have started to remove some of your masks, and you will have started to become aware of many others.

It's an exhilarating time for you, this journey of discovery, this reconnection with your true self, with anticipation of all the new opportunities which can and do start to open up for you as a result! Indeed, in the next section we take a closer look at life beyond your masks - there's a lot there waiting for you.

Before we do that though, we need to consider one very important question.

Will the masks come back?

It's a very good question. After all, who wants to go through all of this, just to have the masks return, perhaps even worse than they were before?

There is both good and bad news in the answer, frustratingly!

The bad news is that yes, it is possible for your masks to return, or for new masks to arrive.

The good news is that you are now in a much better place to stop that from ever happening - provided you are prepared to remain vigilant.

Let us first consider the likelihood of the return of our old masks, the ones of which we are now very much aware.

While it is absolutely possible for these masks to sneak back in to place when we are not looking, the reality is that now that we have become aware of those old masks we are generally much more likely to be able to spot when they might be making a re-appearance. Which means that, if we are on our guard, we can keep them away. By which I mean we just need to keep an eye out for the first signs of those masks returning; the first signs of any of those old avoidance habits starting to come back.

What signs do we need to keep watch for?

Think back to some of the questions we explored earlier, the ones which uncovered those tell-tale signs that we were wearing masks. Pay close attention to those questions, for they highlight the early warning signs that masks may be starting to attempt to reform.

For example, suppose that one of the signs you discovered was that you always strived to keep your hobbies a secret a work. That whenever conversation got round to what you'd each been up to for the weekend, rather than share your hobby, you pretended to have been doing something else - anything else - for fear that you might be ridiculed.

Having now successfully become aware of that mask, and either removed it or at least started on the journey of being able to remove it, you would be well advised to just keep a watchful eye out for any such habit returning. Just notice if there are any times where you find yourself either keeping your hobby secret, or not speaking up when asked, or even where you consider hesitating for a moment - those are all signs of the possible return of that mask. The good news is, of course, that just as it's easier to remove weeds before they get a foothold, so it is much easier to stop the mask from coming back than it was to get rid of it. Just be mindful of the possibilities.

What about the arrival of new masks? Is that possible?

Again, it absolutely is - you are still, after all, the same wonderful human being you always were, and so it is still possible for you to develop new masks if you are not careful.

However, it's those last five words which hold the secret to your power to repel these potential new masks. As with keeping old ones away, it's all about being vigilant, and just keeping an eye on what's going on in your life. Notice if there are areas where you seem hesitant to be you, for example.

Fortunately, there are some simple processes you can use to help guard against old masks returning and new ones appearing. When applied regularly, these will really help in your journey to remaining free from masks.

However, before we look at these, it is worth pausing for a moment to remind ourselves to cut us some slack if (or rather when) we spot new masks developing. Just because we see a new mask starting to appear, doesn't mean we have failed. It doesn't mean we are useless or bad at this, or any of the other ways in which so many of us will beat ourselves up for it.

In fact, noticing a new mask is something we should celebrate - celebrate that our awareness is such that we have spotted this mask, and we can do something about it. This is undoubtedly a Good Thing, because in the past we would not even have been aware it was happening.

We are all human, complete with our fallibilities and our flaws. None of us are perfect, nor will we ever be - and in many ways we are all the better for that.

If we start to berate ourselves for seeing the return of a mask, we are harming ourselves in two ways.

First, we are reinforcing the idea that we are useless - which is never a good thing for us to reinforce.

Second, by reacting badly to seeing a mask, we risk not spotting future ones. What happens is that our unconscious spots the mask and alerts us to it - we then react badly. So, what is our unconscious going to do next time it spots a mask? It's more than likely going to keep quiet. Think about it for a moment. If you bring some bad news to your boss, and your boss shouts at you, has a go at you, blames you, then what are you going to do next time there's some bad news? Chances are, you'll not pass it on - why would you, your boss will just shout at you. Which means the important news does not get passed on, and things inevitably go from bad to worse.

Never shoot the messenger, as the saying so wisely puts it.

So, when we spot the signs that a mask is appearing or even returning, simply notice that we are now aware of the mask, acknowledge that it exists, thank ourselves for being aware, and proceed to remove it.

With that all in mind, let's look at the processes I mentioned earlier which can help us to remain vigilant against the return of any masks, old or new.

What I would recommend is a form of nightly review.

It is easy to do, only takes a couple of moments, and when done consistently the results are very powerful.

You may find it even more powerful to use a small notebook and pen specially for your nightly review. This is less about going back and re-reading them over time (although some people can find that helpful), it's more about the act of writing it down which helps to really cement the progress in the mind. Just as we learn far more by manually writing down notes than we learn by passively listening or even by typing up notes, there is something about the act of manually writing in longhand which really forces the mind to truly "get" what we are learning.

Nightly review is best done when we are in bed, last thing at night, just before we switch the lights off and go to sleep. Partly because that means we are reviewing the entire day, and partly because our unconscious mind will be working on aspects of it as we sleep, which can also help to generate powerful positive results (provided we frame things the right way, of course!).

The nightly review consists of three steps:

1. What, if anything, did I do today which now looks like hiding?
2. What did I do today which was only possible because I had no mask?
3. Celebrate!

Let's look at each of these three steps in a little more detail.

What, if anything, did I do today which now looks like hiding?

For this step, it can be particularly helpful to treat it not as if you are looking back at what you did, but to play the role of a caring supervisor, reviewing your day with you, looking back in a detached manner with the full benefit of hind-sight.

It's absolutely not about apportioning blame, not about finding fault, nor is it about finding things to berate oneself for.

Far from it. It is about taking a few moments to look back over the day, with the full benefit of hindsight, in as detached a way as possible, so see if you can spot any points where you might have been hiding. It's about spotting these tell-tale signs of the potential reappearance of masks early, so that you can address them sooner rather than later.

When you first start this practise, you might find that every night you see no signs of hiding at all. I'd encourage you, at this early stage, to be really curious, and to ask yourself whether there really were no examples, or whether you are perhaps hiding them or are not quite yet fully aware of what you are looking for. Then move on to the next stage anyway, knowing your unconscious mind will look at the situation slightly differently next time you examine it the following evening.

After a little while, as you get better at spotting the signs of hiding, you might find the opposite happens - you start seeing not one but several examples every single day, almost to the point it gets overwhelming!

That's also OK, what is happening is that your unconscious mind is still calibrating and getting used to looking for these examples -

after all, this is probably completely new to you, so it will take a little while to settle in. How long that "little while" is will differ from person to person, and that's absolutely fine. Just go with it, knowing that every day you do this makes you that little bit better at it.

If you do spot lots of examples, acknowledge them, and pick just one to focus upon. How to choose? Pick the one which "feels" right, the one which looks the best one to deal with right now, perhaps the one which resonates most with you.

Pick the one example and have a good look at it. What was going on for you there? How was the mask trying to assert itself? Was there a genuine risk, or was it in hindsight a safe situation where you could be you anyway? What specifically can you learn from that particular situation which will help you next time?

Just spend a few moments pondering that. Don't try to force answers, just go with your instinct, your gut feel, your intuition, whatever you want to call it, and see what comes up. Allow whatever learning wants to make itself known to do so, absorb it, and get curious about how differently you'll act next time.

After a while of doing this, you'll most likely see a drop in the number of examples, as you get better and better at coping with the situations as they arise. Which means it will become easier to spot those few remaining occasions where they do happen.

Above all, keep doing this each night where possible. Vigilance is the key - if you stop doing this because you have a period of not seeing any mask situations, then you simply make it easier for them to start sneaking back unobserved later.

What did I do today which was only possible because I had no mask?

This is a fun one, and the more you do it, the more fun, exciting, and interesting it gets, as well as becoming ever-more powerful.

Have a look back over your day, with the full benefit of hindsight, and spot one example of something you did, which you would not have been able to do, or would not have attempted to do, if you had still been wearing your masks.

As with the first step, many people find it takes a little time at first to spot these things, so just relax and allow it to come to you. The difference between this and the previous step is that there will always be things you do each day which would not have been possible or which you would not have attempted to do had you been wearing masks.

It doesn't have to be something big, either - as is so often the case in life, it can be the smallest of details which makes the important difference.

To give a slightly related example, back in the days when I was working through conquering my social phobia (before I'd refined the tools to make conjuring phobias such a quick process), I remembered one occasion when I was at a hotel for a seminar. I was checking out of the room but was still attending the seminar for the rest of the day and wanted to leave my case somewhere safe. So, I asked, when checking out, about whether there was any way for my luggage to be kept safe. The lady behind the desk said I should speak to the Concierge who would be happy to handle it, and I completed checking out.

I went to try to find the Concierge and could not figure out where they were. Now, previously, being terrified of speaking with strangers, I'd have got a bit worked up about this and panicked about not being able to find them, and worried what I was going to do with my case, and so on. I'd have probably ended up just leaving and going home early (yeah, I know - but that's the power phobias have over us, which is why I find it so rewarding to be able to help people conquer their fears and phobias quickly and permanently).

However, I'd already started to make breakthroughs in my own phobia, and I plucked up the courage to ask someone where Concierge was. They happily pointed me in the right direction, and all was well.

It's a trivial thing to most people - don't know where Concierge is, just ask someone. Pretty obvious and trivial thing to do, right?

But for me, at that time, this was a significant achievement because of my situation. It would absolutely be worth noticing in a nightly review.

So, have a look back over your day, and look for one example of where you did something which you would not have done had you still been wearing your masks.

Just one example is all you need.

Once you have the example, examine it, relive it, notice how good it makes you feel to realise you did this thing, and all because you were not wearing a mask.

Allow yourself a moment or two just to bask in that glow. We rarely allow ourselves the luxury of doing so, which is to our detriment.

Celebrate!

Once you've done your nightly review, and you've seen the positive effects of what you are doing, take a moment or two just to celebrate all that you have achieved. Congratulate yourself on achieving it - no matter how small or big the Thing was, celebrate it, congratulate yourself on the success, and get excited and curious about how the coming days will bring even more opportunities.

Then immediately switch off the light, roll over, and drift off into a wonderful and restful sleep.

This last step is important! Don't do nightly review then jump onto your phone or tablet for a half hour of browsing. Review, celebrate, then go to sleep.

Doing this, you allow your unconscious mind's focus to be on all the positivity and benefits from your nightly review, which in turn allows it to continue looking for, and finding, positivity, which means when you wake up in the morning you are in a much better position to be able to ace your day.

III

BEYOND YOUR MASKS

11

A NEW LIFE

Now that you are aware of masks, aware of some of your own masks, and aware of how to start removing them, it's time to pause for a moment and take a look at the new life which awaits you.

For some, this can be a time of great excitement, at the thought of all the new opportunities which open up for you.

For others, it can be a time of great confusion and even fear, at the prospect of entering the world afresh, having stripped away all the "defence barriers" you previously had in place, and having to figure things out from scratch.

And for perhaps most, it's a mix of both things. I know it was for me as I started to remove my own masks. Part of me was getting excited about all the new things I could do, looking forward to doing things which, for my whole life until that point, had been nothing more than a long-frustrated and unattainable dream. On the other hand, part of me was, not to put too fine a point on it, absolutely terrified. What was I doing? This was completely new territory. I was venturing into areas I'd never even considered before, attempting to do things of which previously I'd only ever dreamed - who was little old me to dare to even think about attempting them?

I get it. I really get it.

All change has the potential to be scary and facing a life free from our comforting and "protective" masks is perhaps just about the biggest voluntary change one can make.

However, with a little forward planning and some careful consideration, we can mitigate the perceived dangers, and start to create our life on our terms. It's rather liberating once you get the hang of it.

The first thing to note is that just because you have now removed (some of) your masks, it doesn't mean that life is plain sailing from this point. I wish I could tell you that it is, but alas nothing in life is ever that straightforward.

Yes, there will be times when you feel a little anxious or even scared. That is a good sign, believe it or not. It shows that you are alive, and it also shows that you are really paying attention to your situation and surroundings.

Remember in chapter 9 "Dealing With The Fear" we saw that fear is something to make friends with, and which can become a very powerful ally. If you have any doubt about this, I strongly suggest you go back and re-read that chapter right now, before going any further. It will help you a lot over the weeks, months, and years ahead.

Yes, there will also be setbacks. Which are nothing more than opportunities to learn, to re-evaluate, and to grow even stronger than before.

So, what of this new life ahead of us? What is it all about, and how can we make sure we are able to take full advantage of it?

There are two parts to this process. They can be summarised simply as:

1. Get in touch with what you truly want from life
2. Make the changes you need to get it

Sounds simple, right?

And in many ways, it is. Just as in many ways people can feel it is really complicated. The actual journey will vary from person to person. Some will find these steps easy to do, others will find they need some help, which is where I come in helping my clients to navigate their way through these steps.

Let's look at what is involved in each of these steps.

GET IN TOUCH WITH WHAT YOU TRULY WANT IN LIFE

We began to touch on some of this in an earlier chapter, so already your unconscious mind is starting to become aware of the possibilities. So, let's take it a little further.

You might already have a good idea of the things you want to do and achieve in life. If so, that's excellent! It's still worth going through this though because you never know quite what you might uncover.

You'll want plenty of blank paper and a pen or two (or lots, if you like to colour-code things as they come to you). Whatever works best for you.

Think back to when you were a child.

What sorts of things did you love doing?

What were your dreams?

What were your hopes and ambitions?

Really take some time to get back in touch with the child you were before you answer. Remember, this version of you has been hidden away for a long time, so it may take a while to really get back in touch.

You might, if it is possible, find it helpful to have a chat with your parents or siblings or even grandparents or aunts or uncles. Ask them about your dreams when you were young. Get really curious about them.

I remember having a chat with my sister a few years ago, and she reminded me of something I'd long forgotten. Apparently when I was about 10 or 11, I was fascinated by hypnosis. I would go around, as 10 years olds do, pretending I had this superpower, and I pretended I could hypnotise people. And apparently, so my sister reminded me, I used to tell people that I would find out how hypnosis works, and I would become a hypnotist.

Of course, life got in the way, and those dreams were long-buried, along with my dreams of being an author or a performer or even a magician - I had a very vivid imagination growing up.

I ended up in a career in IT, as I have mentioned elsewhere, for 20 years.

However, the interesting thing is that once I conquered my shyness and overcame my own phobias, and started to remove my own masks, I started to find myself drawn inexplicably to certain activities. Over recent years I became a hypnotist, an author, a magician, and an entertainer.

Amazing how our childhood reveals our true desires - who we were before society told us who we should be.

I sometimes wonder what would have happened if I'd had that chat with my sister a few years earlier…

But I digress.

Get in touch with the young you, really dig deep, find out what the young you yearned to be, to do. As I mentioned above, if you can't remember the details (which is perfectly natural, after all they have been hidden away for a long time) then have conversations with trusted family members to help unveil them. And write it all down.

Once you've started down this path, often more and more will reveal itself - it's almost as if those inner hopes and dreams and wishes, sensing that they are no longer trapped, start rushing forward.

Write them all down, get curious about how they feel - try them out, imagine fulfilling them, see how that all feels.

Once you feel you've got everything out from this part of the exercise (and yes, it's perfectly OK to take your time and to even come back to it again to see what other long-buried memories start to make themselves known), you can then start to consider how they relate to your current life. Which, if any of them, you would like to start building into your future.

Have a think about the things you really enjoy doing today. What are the things that you enjoy so much that you lose track of time?

Things which, if money were no object, you'd happily do until the end of time because you enjoy them so much.

Now think about things you'd like to do just as much but, for whatever reason you never got round to doing. Most of those reasons will be related to the old masks you used to wear.

Then put it all together - the hopes and dreams of the young you, the things you currently enjoy doing, and the things you'd like to enjoy doing.

Explore them all, mentally try them out, see how they all feel.

Once you've done all of that - and you can take as long as you feel you need to take to explore it all - take a fresh piece of paper and start to describe your ideal life embracing these hopes, desires, dreams, and ambitions.

You might decide to describe a typical day involving them, in great detail (write it as present tense rather than future tense, and make it as descriptive and compelling as you possibly can).

Or if you prefer, you might draw to represent it in whatever way feels right for you - don't worry about the "quality" of the drawings, that's not important. What IS important is to create whatever works before for you.

I have had some clients who have chosen to use other forms of expression - poetry, music, songs, even clay modelling – different methods to suit different people. Just go with whatever feels most fun for you.

The important thing is to get as detailed as you can, and to thoroughly enjoy it all.

Out of all of this, you will start to get an idea of what specifically you want to do with your new life, which leads us neatly on to the second step.

MAKE THE CHANGES YOU NEED TO GET IT - THE SIX STEPS FOR CHANGE

Since I first started helping people to transform their deepest fears into their greatest strengths back in 2010, everything I do is about helping people to CHANGE.

Although any form of change can be scary at times, I've developed a strong 6-step framework for change which gives you the greatest chance for success. It gives you the ability to make the maximum positive change with the minimum necessary effort.

It forms the basis of the work I do with most of my clients, and I thought I'd share it with you here so that you can see how you can implement it in your own areas of change.

Step 1 – Clear the emotion

When we clear the underlying emotions, fear does not get a chance to develop.

Deep down, we are very emotional creatures. We are driven by emotion a lot – we seek to avoid or remove ourselves from situations which make us feel bad and look to find and take part in things which make us feel good. It is this emotion which can hold us back from doing things for fear of experiencing a bad result.

Or sometimes worse, it is emotion we hold about past events which causes us to avoid moving forward in the future.

For example, one client had been laughed at when they sang once at school in front of their classmates – which they carried with them ever since. The result was that despite them being an excellent singer, they could not bring themselves to perform in front of others – the emotion from way back was still affecting them.

We worked together to quickly release that old emotion, and suddenly all previous nerves about performing were permanently banished.

Step 2 – Harness new decisions

We can change the decisions we made in the past and change the results we get.

It may sound strange, but we can change the decisions we made in the past.

This is because nothing which ever happens has an absolute meaning – indeed, nothing has any meaning but that which we ascribe to it.

Something happens to us, we decide it must mean something, and go through life accordingly. But the reality is, it could "mean" whatever we choose it to mean.

Which is why we can change those decisions we made (you know, like "I'm not good enough", "People like me never succeed", "I don't deserve it" etc).

And when we change them, it has a massive effect for our lives for now and our new future.

Step 3 – Align your values

When we align everything we do with everything that's important to us, we dissolve the barriers to our success.

Our values are things which are important to us – for example, they might include loyalty, health, happiness, justice, success, money, equality - in short, anything which is really important to us.

When we attempt to do something which is against our values, or is not supported by our values, then we create so many more artificial and real barriers to our own success.

By bringing everything we do in line with everything that is important to us (as well as addressing any conflicts within what is important to us), the two work together to propel us through any barrier we may think we face.

Step 4 – Notice your skill gaps

Often the biggest barrier to our success is knowing which skills we need.

Once we have cleared out the old emotional responses and the old disempowering decisions which were holding us back, and once we have aligned our values and our desired outcomes, the next step is to take stock of where we want to go, what skills we need to take us there, and compare those against our existing skills (and knowledge).

By doing this, we can quickly identify those areas which we need to develop our skills or knowledge.

It is important to do this only after the first three steps, of course, so that we are not being artificially held back.

Step 5 – Gain your new skills

Once you know what you need to know, gaining those skills brings about massive results, very quickly.

Once you know which skills you need to gain, it becomes merely a matter of finding out how you can learn them, and then polishing them.

You might look to enrol in a local college, or to hire a coach or mentor in those areas, or to do your own self-study and research.

Or you might even ask friends or others who already have those skills, and find out what they do, how they do it, and study them to figure it out.

Step 6 – Engage your new life

Once you have made changes and put these new things in place, it's time to truly engage with your new life and live it the way you always wanted to.

Engage in those new skills, following those new dreams, achieving those new goals.

Remembering, of course, that this is a process of constant measuring and checking to see that you are on course and to adjust course accordingly. The beauty here is that you are no longer wondering whether you can do something, you are too busy enjoying the process of making the journey itself work.

This is the 6-step model I have used to make my own changes to my life, and which I use with clients to help them to make massively successful changes in their lives.

You are welcome to use this same model for the changes you want to make in your own life, or if you'd prefer then you and I can use it together to help you to make the changes you want to make. The decision is yours - whether you decide to go it alone, or decide we should work on it together, all that I ask is that you DO make the changes you want in life.

Make the changes now that your future self will thank you for. After all, you've got rid of the masks, it would be a shame to waste this new-found potential at this stage.

12

8 POWERFUL WORDS

Once you really get rid of all your masks, and get used to living life without them, and keep them off, then you really start to enter a much more empowered way of life.

You start to live life free from concerns about what "others" will think of you.

You start to live life on your own terms, being true to who you are.

You start to see, and take, the opportunities which only arise once you are truly free from others' judgements and expectations.

As you start to truly live life without masks, you start to experience a life free from judgement by others, free from exceptions of others, from the fear of letting others down. You can concentrate on life on your own terms, doing what you truly and passionately believe is the right thing to do. It is an incredibly liberating and empowering place in which to be.

And as you truly embrace this new-found way of living, and keep those masks well away, so you start to embody the 8 Powerful Words which really make all the difference.

This is me; this is who I am

It is important to be aware that these words are not coming from a place of ego or pride or anger or challenge.

We are absolutely not saying "This is me; this is who I am, and if you don't like it then you can just clear off because you are wrong" (or words to that effect - you get the general idea).

Indeed, if those words do come from such a place, if there is anger or ego or pride associated with them, then one is absolutely not embodying the words at all.

These 8 Powerful Words are coming simply from a place of quiet acceptance. It's merely a statement of fact, free from all emotion or ego or pride or desire to prove anything or to challenge anyone. It's the opposite of challenge. It is simply saying that what you see with me is what you get with me. That I don't hide anything, that I don't pretend to be what I'm not, that I won't change to please others, I am just me.

This is me; this is who I am

It also comes with the implicit understanding and unconditional acceptance that the same is true for everyone else.

When you fully embrace and embody "This is me; This is who I am" you are implicitly offering an invitation to anyone who likes you. You are implying that it would be cool to hang out together some time, and to see what magic you can work together in this wonderful world, but just each being yourself and timing up to unite your strengths.

You are also offering words to those who would dislike you - you are implying that you and they will probably never hang out, and that's OK. Further, you are wishing them all the best, and hoping that they will find the people who they do like so that they can hang out together and create their magic for the world.

You are recognising that just as you are who you are, so they are who they are, and that's fine in both cases. Neither is wrong, each is right in their own way, and all is as it should be with the world.

This is me; this is who I am

Think about building a house. You need lots of different things to come together to make it work. Floor, walls, doors, windows, roof, tiles, plumbing, electrical wiring, insulation, paint, the list goes on.

Each thing is different.

Some combinations can be extremely dangerous and deadly, yet other combinations are beautifully harmonious.

And every single one of those components are required - remove any one of them, and you don't have a house. Try to build a house using ONLY one of them, and you don't get very far - imagine a house built entirely out of light-switches, for example!

It's the same for building a car, or creating a computer, or building absolutely anything, large or small. It only works because different components each bring their own strengths and weaknesses, and work together as a whole by pooling their strengths and covering each other's weaknesses.

Just as a sheet of glass would make for a very fragile engine block, so a block of aluminium would make a very poor window. Yet swap their use round, and…

And so, it is with people, too.

This is me; this is who I am

We are all different, we all have different strengths, weaknesses, attitudes, abilities… the list goes on. It's no wonder that not everyone likes everyone else as there are so many different and often seemingly incompatible combinations.

However, that is where the 8 Powerful Words can help so much.

By recognising that we are who we are and that is OK, and by also recognising that every other individual is who they are and that is OK too, we enable ourselves to continue to be fully us, without compromise or fear of judgement, and we afford others the same courtesy.

This is me; this is who I am

All of which enables each one of us, ultimately, to bring our strengths to the fore, to enable us all to utilise each strength, to cover for each other's weaknesses. All of which is for the overall good of humanity. Indeed, ultimately, it paves the way for the elevation of a united human race to its next level of growth, development, and consciousness.

Which sounds like a rather lofty claim, and in some ways it is. However, it is the inevitable and, let's face it, highly desirable, result when all of us can fully embrace and embody those 8 Powerful Words.

This is me; this is who I am

And meantime, until that happens, we can simply embrace the 8 Powerful Words and know that by so doing we are enabling ourselves to live our best life, and at the same time as we saw as far back as chapter 3, we are inspiring others to be open to living their best lives - including inspiring many who we may never actually meet, many of whom we may never even hear. By being true to ourselves, but living life without masks, by shining bright like a beacon, we give those other people hope, encouragement, and permission to be themselves, to ditch their masks, and to live their best lives.

This is me; this is who I am

A USEFUL ANCHOR

At this point, I would like to off you an anchor which I have found really helps me to keep the masks off, especially in times where I might be tempted to temporarily wear a mask "just this once" (which, of course, would never be just the once...).

Before I do, I should probably explain what an anchor is - we're not talking in a nautical context here.

In this context, an anchor is something which triggers a thought or memory or emotional response.

Perhaps the smell of delicious freshly baked bread brings back wonderful childhood memories.

Or hearing a particular piece of music brings back a memory of a particular moment in time in a relationship and rekindles all the emotions that go along with that memory.

Even wearing particular clothes, or doing particular actions, can work well as anchors. For example, I know of professional speakers who always step on to their stage in a particular way, because they have used that to create an anchor to bring them into their preferred best emotional state for delivering their talk. I know of professional sports people who will undertake a particular ritual every time just before performing, because they have used that to create a positive powerful anchor to hype themselves up into peak performance.

Anchors come from the work that Ivan Pavlov did with his dogs - yes *that* Pavlov and *those* dogs. For those who are not familiar with this, while he was developing his study of digestion in dogs (work which ultimately lead to him winning a Nobel Prize in 1904) he noticed something interesting. He noticed that after a while, the dogs would start to salivate every time an assistance entered the room. Not because the dogs were salivating at the thought of eating the poor assistant, it should be pointed out. What Pavlov discovered was that because the assistants had always brought the food in, the dogs started to associate the assistants with food, and so even when they did not actually bring any food in with them, the dogs would still salivate. They had developed what would go on to be called a Conditioned Response, which is what an Anchor is.

(You might at this point be asking "Wait a minute, didn't Pavlov ring bells?". It turns out this is a very common and popular idea but is unfortunately a misconception. He did go on to study what was happening with his dogs in greater detail, but he used a metronome rather than a bell).

OK, that's all very interesting, but what does this have to do with keeping our masks away, you may very well be wondering?

Well, by complete accident, I stumbled upon an incredibly powerful anchor which really helps me to avoid the return of masks. I thought I'd share mine, in the hopes that you might discover an anchor which works equally well for you.

For me, it goes back to a very early memory that I've always had, and until recently never really knew why.

It was Christmas Day and I was three. I'd got a go kart for Christmas, and that afternoon we were in the sitting room. I was sat in my go kart, my baby sister sat on my knee, and I have always had a very vivid memory of this exact moment, me sat there looking straight at my Dad who was stood in front with a camera. Being the 1960s it used one of those big flashguns with the flashbulb that you can only use once. So, I have always remembered being sat there, looking straight at my Dad and thus at the camera, while he set the shot up and took the photo.

Never knew why, but I always remembered that photo being taken (no others, just that one).

And then a few years ago, my Mum and I were flicking through an old family photo album. We turned the page and there it was. I came face-to-face with that very photograph. The one I'd always remembered being taken.

As I looked at the photo, I was overcome with a very strange, powerful, and deeply moving feeling. I was staring straight at the photo, and the three-year-old me was staring straight out of the photo (I'd been looking directly at the camera, as instructed at the time). I was gazing into three-year-old me eyes. It was as if three-year-old me and current me were reaching across time, connecting with each other across the years, forming a very deep bond. I was instantly reconnected with the three-year-old me. The me who was ME, long before society had told me who I should be. I was instantly reconnected with all the warmth, joy, expectation of three-year-old me.

It's hard to describe, but it was such a powerful experience. All from looking at a black-and-white photo.

However, it's that photo which has given me such a powerful anchor..

Any time I am ever in a situation where I might feel the temptation to hide a little, to pretend not to be me, to wear a mask, I just think of that photo. I take a moment to remember the photo, to really see it in my mind's eye, and to gaze into the eyes of that three-year-old me. As I do that, as I reconnect with the real inner me, any thoughts of wearing any sort of mask, however temporary, all melt away completely. After all, how could I possibly deny that inner me? How could I ever knowingly force it to wear any sort of mask ever again?

That is my anchor which really helps if I am ever in a potential mask situation.

My hope is that, as you remove your masks and get used to a mask-free life, you will uncover your own anchor which helps you to keep in touch with the real you, and thus helps you to avoid masks.

Obviously, your anchor will be different from mine - everyone's will be different, unique, based upon their own experience and needs. And, I express the sincere hope that you will find one, sooner or later.

It might be some new experience you have which really cements life without a mask for you. Or it might be a dawning realisation of the meaning of a previous experience, now viewed from this fresh perspective, taking on a deeper significance for you.

Whatever it turns out to be for you, I hope you enjoy it and find it helpful over the years ahead.

14

WHEN IS A MASK NOT A MASK?

Whenever I give my "8 Powerful Words" talk, upon which this book is based, in the ensuing lively and informative discussion there is a question which arises more than any other. It's such a common, and insightful, question that it really does deserve its very own chapter.

The specific wording varies each time of course, but the underlying basis of the question remains the same, and concerns wondering whether there are times where it is better for all concerned if we wear a mask.

A typical example might be that when we are in a corporate business setting, there is a certain expectation in terms of behaviour, language, even attire. If we dress up in whatever is deemed to be a corporate professional outfit, and if we act in particular ways because we know that is what is expected, rather than rocking up in t-shirt and shorts and using our usual "colourful" language, doesn't that mean we are wearing a mask?

If we take our mask off in such situations, isn't that going to cause us all problems?

It's certainly an interesting question, and at first glance it might seem that we are wearing masks in those situations.

However, there is a big difference.

A mask is something we wear, usually unconsciously (as if we are not even aware we are wearing it - we may never have been aware of it even when it first slid insidiously onto us). It is something we may be wearing most of the time, only letting it slip on occasions where we've managed to start to feel it is safe, although even then we may still be on our guard.

In many cases, we wear it the entire time, so much so that we even start to fool ourselves into believing it is who we are.

Which is where their danger comes, as we've seen throughout this book already.

However, that is very different from the example being raised here, namely of the business person behaving in a particular manner because it is expected.

In this scenario, they are very much aware of what they are doing, and they are actively trying to behave, dress, speak in this manner.

So, what is going on?

It is important to remember that each one of us are complex people with multiple facets to our personalities, and with different behaviours depending upon our situation.

For example, one might be very serious, contentious, commanding of respect, and highly focused and disciplined at work. Whereas when chilling a home with the family, one might be completely different - relaxed, goofy, paying scant attention to the minutiae of the details, etc. One will have one set of behaviours when playing with one's young child, and a very different set of behaviours when alone in the bedroom with one's spouse.

None of which are masks.

They are simply different facets of our personality coming to the fore, depending upon the situation. In each situation, we are still very much us, the core of our being remains uncompromised.

Then we also have the various rules and conventions which we all follow to make life that little bit smoother.

Any time two or more people interact, there has to be certain rules to facilitate a harmonious - or at the very least to reduce the risk of a dangerous and unpleasant - interaction.

We have a whole host of spoken rules, of protocols, of rituals, all of which have evolved over the centuries or millennia, all to help us to get along with our fellow humans.

We observe these social niceties because it is in our mutual interests so to do. We each know we are following the "rules", there is no pretence about it, there's no hiding behind masks - just a mutual acceptance that this particular dance is the time-honoured way to carry out this interaction.

All of which is very much not a mask. It is not something behind which we are hiding. We are not pretending to be someone we are not. We are not unaware that we are hiding our true selves. We are simply doing what it takes to make the interaction as please and productive for everyone as is possible.

Even things like basic good manners count here.

Smiling sweetly and saying "Don't mention it" when someone apologises for stepping on your foot, when you actually want to shout "Watch where you are **** going you idiot!" isn't wearing a mask, it's simply recognising that a little politeness is the best course of action all round in this situation.

Why is any of this relevant?

The reason it's important to discuss it, is that sometimes when they think of being wholly free from masks, some people feel this gives them the excuse, indeed the right, to do what they want when they want regardless of anyone else around.

Which is absolutely not the case at all.

Remember back to the 8 Powerful Words - "This is me; this is who I am".

Remember that we observed that this is not coming from a place of pride or ego or challenge. Instead, it is coming from a place of quiet acceptance that we are who we are- and that applies to all of us, including the other people around us.

This is me; this is who I am - and you are you, you are who you are. Neither of us is inherently right or wrong about anything, we each are who we each are, and in both cases who we are is worthy of respect from the other for it.

It is as much about honouring the other person for who they are, as it is about accepting ourselves for who we are.

Which means that if the customs of the situation require that we wear a suit, then we simply wear a suit and get on with it. None of which means we are hiding behind any masks. Indeed, by having no masks at all, we are even more able to be comfortably us even when we need to wear a suit or act according to particular social conventions and expectations where the situation demands.

This is me, this is who I am. I am someone who is perfectly comfortable with observing the traditions and customs which society has evolved, because I know it does not impact who I am, I know it simply enables you and I to interact effectively and with minimum impediment.

15

WHERE TO NOW?

Congratulations!

You have been on quite a journey, so it's time to look a look at what is next for you in life.

Before we do that, it is very useful just to take a moment to pause and reflect on all that you have achieved so far, and to celebrate it.

You have achieved what so many people fail to even be aware of.

Over the course of working your way through this book, you have:

- Become aware of what masks are, how we develop them, and the massive damage they do.
- Become aware of your own masks, the ones you've been wearing for so long in life.
- Removed those masks - perhaps not all of them yet, but you have started removing many of them, and no doubt you can continue to remove the remaining masks over the coming days, weeks, and months.

- Developed powerful defences against new masks appearing, or old ones returning.
- Got in touch with some of your life's dreams, goals, and ambitions, and started to dare once more to dream of a world where you follow and even achieve these.

That is a lot. And it is definitely worth celebrating.

So I invite you, right here, right now, to take a few moments to just look back over this, to reflect on what you've already achieved, to make sure you are fully aware of how far you have come already, and to take a few moments to really congratulate yourself on everything so far.

Go on, I'll wait.

OK, now you've celebrated, it's time to get curious and excited about your future.

Of course, we've already started to have a glimpse of what this new life might be, and hopefully got excited about the possibilities.

So now it's time to focus on the practicalities, the Next Steps.

They will differ from person to person, of course. There is no one-size-fits-all, not single Right Thing that will work for everyone. That's all part of the fun of life, figuring out what is right for you.

If you've worked through all the chapters in order before reaching this one, then you'll already have a fair idea of the sorts of things you want to do.

Picking your next step is often the most difficult part of the process, and one of the most important.

Take some time to get clear on what you want to do, what you want to achieve.

Get clear on what and who you need to be to achieve them.

Take a good look at the six step process for CHANGE outlined in chapter 11. Really pay close attention to that process, as it will absolutely guide you to what to do next. It will help you create your plan of action.

Some people can start those next steps on their own.

Other people find they need some help and encouragement from family and friends.

And yet others find they benefit from some help from a coach or other outside resource.

Whichever approach feels right for you, embrace it fully, and really go for it.

Whatever you decide to do in life, I wish you the very best of success - I hope you have the most amazing, wonderful, happy, and above all mask-free life it is possible to have.

I'd love to hear how you've got on, what this journey together has meant for you - please do feel free to drop me an email and let me know what you've learned about yourself, what your new future looks like. I'd love to read it and share a little in your success, so do drop me a line - you'll find my contact details at the back of the book.

Thank you for coming on this journey with me, I hope you have found it a rewarding and enjoyable one.

Take care, look after yourself, and until our paths cross again remember that change is always possible; and when you change your mind, you change your life.

EPILOGUE

So, what of my life after that realisation that I am gay? And what of the life of my then wife? Naturally, it meant the end of our marriage, to the ultimate benefit of both of us. Yes, it was sad that it ended, but I am happy to report that we ended things in an amicable and equitable manner - after all, we were both the same people we'd always been deep down. Fortunately, we had no children so that made things far simpler. We opted for a "DIY divorce", filling out the forms together and filing them with the local Crown Court to petition for divorce on the grounds of irreconcilable differences after a period of separation.

I can remember the day we filed the petition with the court. We both met up in town, I had the papers with me, we both signed them, walked to the court together and handed them in, then headed off into town to grab a bite to eat together as it was lunchtime. We had a very pleasant chat, then went our separate ways.

I am very pleased to be able to report that we have remained in contact over the years since. We now live at opposite ends of the country - not by design, that's just where our lives have taken each of us, but we still exchange the occasional greeting. She, I am absolutely delighted to report, is very happily remarried with a most wonderful husband, and they have been together for a great many years - hopefully they will be happily married together for a great many more to come. Obviously, I am going in to no more detail, for theirs is not my story to tell.

As for me? Well, I've been through all manner of adventures since then - there's the epic adventure in Nepal and Tibet, or the year and a half in Bali, or there's the time I was training people in hypnosis at the Great Hall in Coopers Union, NYC, or the time I was kidnapped in Vietnam, or the 20 year career in IT with so many opportunities to observe human behaviour, or a great many other stories, but perhaps let's save those for another time.

However, they have all helped shape who I am, and have ultimately led me to the realisations about some of my own masks, and to removing those of which I am aware.

Have I got rid of all my masks?

Probably not - I say that because I rather suspect all of us will have various deep masks of which perhaps, we may never become aware.

However, I can say, hand on heart, that I have become aware of, and I have successfully removed, a lot of very significant masks. Yes, it has sometimes been a scary journey (although it would have been rather easier if I'd had this book to ready 30 years ago), but very much a worthwhile one.

A journey on which I am still travelling, and undoubtedly will until I draw my final breath, but for now I feel I have removed certainly the biggest, deepest, and strongest masks, and right now I do feel that I can truthfully say that my name is Keith Blakemore-Noble, I am the UK's #1 Fear Strategist, this is me, and this is who I am.

NEED A LITTLE HELP?

By reading and working through this book you have already made many changes, which is getting you off to a fantastic start.

As your journey continues, you might find you have everything you need, and that you have access to all the resources and support you'll need, to enable you to do what you want to do. In which case I wish you every success with your journey.

On the other hand, like many (or perhaps even most) people, you might find there are times in life where you feel you might benefit from some help - some additional guidance, insight, or other assistance.

If this is you, then you are most definitely not alone - you are probably in the majority. Should you decide to seek help, then here are some of the ways that I have helped people like you in similar situations. Have a look, see which ones resonate with you, and do get in touch - it would be my honour and pleasure to be able to help you to continue this amazing journey which you have started.

FORWARD THROUGH FORGIVENESS

Sometimes, despite our best attempts, we find ourselves held back by being unable to let go of emotional attachment and baggage from the past. Forward Through Forgiveness is an online self-paced program designed to enable you to completely let go, and to move on by letting go.

FREEDOM FROM PHOBIA

Whether it's a phobia or a fear that's holding you back, this session will help you to completely conquer it once and for all. It is effectively my signature product, and is available as either a personal 1-2-1 session (usually via Zoom), or as a self-paced online program - either way, it enables you to conquer your phobia or fear quickly and permanently.

LIFE AFTER PHOBIA

For those who know they need to conquer that fear and who also want to then build the life they desire afterwards, this combines Freedom From Phobia with a three month intensive life coaching program designed specifically for your needs, where you and I work together, 1-2-1, to create your life after phobia.

PERSONAL BREAKTHROUGH

Described as the ultimate in personal coaching, this is a full-on intensive whole-day 1-2-1 session where you and I work together (usually via Zoom) to enable you to make a complete breakthrough in your chosen area of life. Together we analyse your situation, elicit what you want, uncover what's stopping you, and blast through those blockages, fine-tuning your mindset to enable you to truly go for it.

STRATEGY SESSION

Sometimes you just need to sit down for an hour and to brainstorm strategy to help you figure out what specifically you need to do next, and to create your plan of action. That's what this session is all about. You and me on Zoom for one hour, creating the strategy you need to follow to achieve your next step. You'll leave with a workable plan of action to get you where you want to go.

You can find out further details about all of these (and more) by going to KeithBlakemoreNoble.com/services - and if you quote "Masks" when you order, or tell me you have this book, you'll get 10% off as a thank you for reading it - perfect!

ABOUT THE AUTHOR

Keith Blakemore-Noble is a coach, international speaker, best-selling author, hypnotist, trainer, podcaster, and occasional magician.

He helps people to transform their deepest fears into their greatest strengths - since 2010 he has helped over 5,000 people across the planet to transform their lives, which is why he is the UK's #1 Fear Strategist.

From paralysing shyness to teaching on stages in the UK, USA, Indonesia, Vietnam, Malaysia, and Singapore, Keith has come far from a life that is just a distant memory now. He has been described as someone who brings a natural humour and wit to the stage, and a captivating presence, allowing you to learn from him with ease as he shares with you the same tools which he used to make massive transformations in his own life and those of his clients.

A living embodiment of the cutting-edge sciences and tools he employs, he has used them all on himself first, so he knows how well they work and understands how the processes feel from your perspective.

Prior to moving full-time into helping people, he spent the best part of two decades in IT, including leading a team with members in the UK, Norway, and New Zealand. He has gone from reprogramming and upgrading computers to reprogramming and upgrading people's minds. The latter is infinitely more rewarding, it must be said.

An accomplished international speaker, Keith has spoken for a wide variety of organisations including the BBC, 4Networking, Rotary International, BNI, and more, on topics around confidence, fear, phobias, and hypnosis.

As well as being the author of this book, he is the mastermind behind the four-volume (so far) international best-selling *"Winning In Life And Work"* series of books, and is already working on his next book for publication in 2021, this time all about phobias.

A strong believer that change is always possible, he invites you to change your mind, and change your life.

Whether it's to approach him for coaching, to book him as a speaker for your next event, or just to find out more about him in general, you could do worse than pop along to his website Keith BlakemoreNoble.com or you can find him across social media under the same name.

Lightning Source UK Ltd.
Milton Keynes UK
UKHW020635190920
370179UK00008B/201